SUPERFOOD
SMOOTHIES

100 DELICIOUS, ENERGIZING &
NUTRIENT-DENSE RECIPES

SUPERFOOD SMOOTHIES

JULIE MORRIS

author of *Superfood Kitchen*

STERLING
New York

STERLING
New York

An Imprint of Sterling Publishing
387 Park Avenue South
New York, NY 10016

Library of Congress Cataloging-in-Publication Data

Morris, Julie (Chef)
   Superfood smoothies : 100 delicious, energizing & nutrient-dense recipes / Julie Morris.
      pages cm
   Includes bibliographical references and index.
   ISBN 978-1-4549-0559-2 (hardback)
   1. Cooking. 2. Functional foods. 3. Health. I. Title.
   TX714.M6773 2013
   641.5--dc23

                    2012046942

              ISBN 978-1-4549-0559-2
         Distributed in Canada by Sterling Publishing
       c/o Canadian Manda Group, 165 Dufferin Street
             Toronto, Ontario, Canada M6K 3H6
     Distributed in the United Kingdom by GMC Distribution Services
   Castle Place, 166 High Street, Lewes, East Sussex, England BN7 1XU
       Distributed in Australia by Capricorn Link (Australia) Pty. Ltd.
             P.O. Box 704, Windsor, NSW 2756, Australia

For information about custom editions, special sales, and premium and corporate purchases,
please contact Sterling Special Sales at 800-805-5489 or specialsales@sterlingpublishing.com.

Manufactured in the United States of America

              4 6 8 10 9 7 5

www.sterlingpublishing.com

CONTENTS

I can still remember that day: On the seventh lap of a 12½ lap, 5km race, I had nothing left. The pack of runners pulled away, leaving me behind. This was certainly not the high school track-and-field debut I was hoping for.

Something wasn't working.

During my training, I had placed my faith in a newly adopted plant-based nutrition plan I created. After trying a wide array of so-called performance diets (everything from high carb–low protein to high protein–low fat to high carb–low fat), I decided to go a simpler, more rounded route. I eliminated all animal products from my meals, a tactic I had been curious about trying for years. I had convinced myself it was going to give me a competitive edge, but obviously the opposite was proving to be true. But why? Why had switching over to a plant-based diet resulted in this energy shortfall?

As I would later discover, it was because I had become a "starch-etarian," as opposed to a vegetarian. I was filling up on nutrient-absent calories by subsisting almost exclusively on starchy processed foods—white bread, pasta, baked goods—while eating almost no vegetables, protein sources, or foods rich in essential fatty acids, and minimal amounts of fruit. While I was certainly getting enough calories and filling up at meals, I was not receiving enough nutrients. As I learned, food is not synonymous with nutrition. In fact, it became clear to me that a common problem in our society was the consumption of increasingly larger portions, while still lacking adequate nutrient intake. Being overfed yet undernourished might have been a paradox as recently as thirty years ago, but not anymore. It has become the new standard, thanks to the refined products that comprise the vast majority of our food supply in North America.

As I would come to realize, breaking down a large volume of refined food for little or no nutritional return is a waste of energy, pure and simple. As you know, when you spend something, you no longer have it. And that was my problem on the track—too much spent energy. So what was the solution? Aside from taking encapsulated supplements, which was a more processed approach, what was the easiest way to get the nutrients that my performance depended upon?

On a whim, I gathered a collection of the most nutrient-dense plant-based and whole food ingredients I could find, added water, and blended it all together. It didn't taste very good, as you can imagine. But every day after my workout, I would scarf down this concoction. It worked. Within a few weeks I was feeling back to normal. After a couple more weeks I felt better than normal, and my escalating performance reflected that. I was able to train more, which translated to greater results, sooner. My blender experiment had convinced me: Nutrition could help me turn triathlons from a hobby into a career. The formula for my daily blended drink continued to evolve over the years, eventually morphing into a commercial version called Vega One. With the nutritional support of my daily smoothie, my career as an athlete advanced at a rapid pace, from running a 2 hour and 29 minute marathon to being victorious in two Canadian National 50km Ultramarathons. Clocking in with the second-fastest run in the world (for a year at least) after I won my second ultramarathon and then beginning my career as a professional Ironman triathlete solidified my confidence in this nutrition and training program.

Like many, my natural athletic ability is average, and in the quest to increase my physical prowess, I found several innovative training techniques that help. However, nutrition has the greatest impact by far. And that's where *Superfood Smoothies* comes in. Not only does Julie work the most nutrient-dense ingredients—superfoods—into her smoothies, she makes them taste good. Really good. As a natural food chef, Julie applies her culinary skills to ensure function meets flavor. Take the Creamy Orange smoothie, for example (a personal favorite): It's packed with health benefits such as essential fats, vitamin E, and anti-inflammatory agents, yet it tastes like a decadent ice cream.

Following Julie's recipes is a holistic and tasty way to reap your full potential, athletically or otherwise. If a resource like this had existed when I was in high school, I would have been on the right track from the beginning.

—*Brendan Brazier*

INTRODUCTION

This story starts in the summertime, when drinking straws took on a whole new meaning for me.

It was a typical Los Angeles July: hot and cranky, the blazing sun filtering the whole city though an orange glow. As a lanky 14-year-old with an unfortunate penchant for ill-fitting, baggy shirts, my schedule for the summer break was nebulously planned with the goal of simply filling time, the quintessential luxury of unaware teenage youth. In the midst of the heavy heat that the San Fernando Valley (yes, *like*, the SoCal "val-eeee") likes to slather on, the long days were passed swimming until I achieved "raisin finger" status, making many—oh so many—trips to the mall, learning the painful lesson that girls with naturally curly hair should never cut their own bangs, and discovering smoothies.

A new chain of smoothie shops had just started popping up and, despite being in a city already overflowing with places to imbibe, this new "blended" business venture was met with quite the local buzz. In what I now see as kismet, this chain (now quite famous, with thousands of locations nationwide) opened one of its very first stores down the street from my house. The menu options were enticingly overwhelming, and no matter how many times I went there, it was always difficult to decide what to order. I would crane my head back and squint at the mile-long list of fruity, frosty, creamy, whipped, magical blends—all while self-consciously distracted by my flustered teenage crush on the smoothie boys behind the counter. I say "boys" as in *all* of them. It didn't seem fair that I had to decide not only between strawberry, apple, mango, banana, or a citrus concoction that tasted like the definition of "wonderful" . . . but also between the impossibly bronzed surfer boy, the artsy-looking one with a nose ring, or Mr. Signature Backward Orange Hat with the bluest eyes ever. Armed only with false confidence, humbled by an obvious blush, and gripping rumpled cash from my parents (who I had desperately pleaded to stay in the car while I ordered), I would awkwardly place my order for, "I don't know, like, maybe the creamy peanut butter one? I forget what it's called." This was the smoothie that tasted like the icebox cookies I was only able to score at the house of a friend with "cool" parents (the ones who understood that junk food was essential to teenage development). "Healthy" was not a word in my vocabulary back then, and smoothies were exclusively a pleasure-based experience.

Cupping the large, heavy, smoothie-filled Styrofoam container (my apologies, environment, I didn't know)—complete with a straw with the paper wrapping still unbroken on top—produced a level of deep-rooted satisfaction usually reserved for much more profound, interesting life events. I would sip away the rest of the afternoon, lost in a frosty bliss that made me forget about the boys for a while. With the dreaded sound of the last slurp, I would begin to plan which flavor I would get on my next visit.

And it wasn't just me. That summer, smoothies became an activity to lure friends over, and utterly trumped our previous family ritual of going out for frozen yogurt. Sometimes my mom, dad, and I would even have smoothies for dinner, and my dad would talk about moving up north and opening his own smoothie shop.

As you can imagine, when I first began reading about the health benefits of drinking smoothies, I instantly thought I had already mastered the art during my Valley girl summers spent hydrated by trucker-sized cups full of the blended concoctions. But I quickly learned that while those early drinks may have technically met the definition of a smoothie, they were far from living up to their health-improving potential. I came to understand that, although the smoothies I was buying were indeed a step above frozen yogurt (or other, far worse desserts), they were also filled with sherbets and heavy on fruit juices (on top of "some" fruit)—all in all, a giant amount of sugar. What a missed opportunity in all those empty calories!

As a chef who specializes in superfoods, I realized that not only could smoothies easily lose their naughty components without a loss in flavor, but they could also gain some amazing nutrition in the mix. The same incredible superfood ingredients I was so passionate about using in my other recipes were absolutely begging to jump into the blender and bestow their benefits to a smoothie. And it was all . . . So. Incredibly. Easy.

When I began to introduce these improved smoothie recipes to friends, family, and clients, the response was universal: "I could drink this every day." Needless to say, I know the feeling well.

Superfood smoothies are empowering. If ever there was a shortcut to taking charge of your health, this is it. The beautiful freshness of the ingredients that go in your blender and the rainbow of goodness that will soon become a part of you are as exciting as they are invigorating. Try to mask your smug smile as you whip an epic blend together in less than a minute. Listen to the promising glug as a freshly poured smoothie fills the glass. If you can, treat yourself to a straw, just because straws make life more fun (I love the reusable glass ones that are available these days). Revel in that first sip, and bask in the superfood smoothie experience—your body certainly is.

Cheers,
Julie

PART ONE

GLOWING BY THE GLASSFUL

To date, no one yet has succumbed to cliché and actually asked me if my cup was half empty or half full. If anyone ever does, and I happen to be lucky enough to be holding a superfood smoothie, I have the perfect retort: My dear, this cup is packed.

SMOOTHIES: THE PERFECT FORM FOR FUNCTION

Few types of food are more nutritious than superfood smoothies. When I look at an empty blender, I see a vessel of health-giving opportunity, ready and waiting to load in as much nutrient-dense goodness as can fit. Fruits? Vegetables? Seeds? Superfoods? Nature tastes just a little better blended.

Like any person working in the culinary field, I've had a fair number of kitchen disasters: ill-seasoned vegetables; pancakes that could have been reused as Frisbees; crusty brownies that clung to the baking pan so emphatically that, even after aggressive scrubbing, they demanded to accompany it all the way to the trash can.

Smoothies, on the other hand, are relaxingly fixable. A smoothie of "eh" status can be transformed into perfection through the simple addition of an extra apple, a spoonful of lemon zest, or even a little chocolate. Although a good smoothie recipe—like any good recipe—is a fleeting piece of well-balanced art, the best smoothies are often made with Jackson Pollock–like enthusiasm, throwing in what feels right and celebrating the organic energy. Once you acquire a small superfood pantry and understand a few core smoothie concepts, the rest easily falls into place.

I hope this book serves as a wonderful inspiration for you, and that you are able to take the 100 gorgeous recipes found in these pages and turn them into 1,000 stunning concoctions of your own. That's part of the beauty of smoothies—they can be tailored and tweaked and personalized infinitely. Today's "best-ever" is tomorrow's "what if we add _____." With their reliance on whole, natural, flavorful foods, smoothies come in a rainbow of colors and tastes, creating the dreamiest desserts or the most refreshing rejuvenators. There's not a favorite flavor around that can't be incorporated into a smoothie.

This book takes that delicious diversity one step further, aiming to pack maximum nutrition into each sip through the use of superfoods. Superfoods, defined as the most nutrient-dense, benefit-rich foods on the planet, deliver a ton of nutritional bang for every caloric buck, and are a profoundly efficient way to realize optimal health benefits in a concentrated form. Their inclusion takes our irresistible natural smoothie bases and catapults them into rich nutritional landscapes, with benefits that would make a vitamin or supplement pill cry with envy.

On top of all these virtues, superfood smoothies couldn't be easier to make. They take minutes—if that. When was the last time you were able to prepare such a profoundly well-rounded, nutrient-rich, mind-blowingly delicious meal or snack so quickly from scratch? That's why smoothies are always the first thing I recommend when I'm asked how to start incorporating superfoods as part of a daily routine.

I also love the social versatility of smoothies. They can be enjoyed by anyone and everyone—from true foodies to the pickiest of eaters to people with special dietary needs—helping all of us reach our health goals. Whether your diet is already exquisitely dialed in and you're just looking for an extra boost, or you want to get healthier but don't know where to begin, superfood smoothies *will* enhance your health and energy either way. They are the easiest way to a stronger, cleaner, more awesome you. How fun!

SUPERFOOD SMOOTHIE PRINCIPLES

To say that not all smoothies are created equal is something of an understatement. As I hinted at in my anecdote in the introduction of this book, just about anything can be blended together and called a smoothie, for better or for worse. This includes excitingly nutritious foods—like super healthy leafy greens and oft-avoided veggies such as beets (which we'll go into more in the upcoming pages)—as well as, unfortunately, some typical dessert ingredients like ice cream and sugar. I've even seen smoothie recipes calling for cake as an ingredient! I'm sure these concoctions are unbearably delicious, and I am not immune to ice cream lust, but as you probably gathered, these examples are not what could be considered superfood smoothies . . . not by a long shot.

On the other hand, I'm sure you're familiar with the many smoothie recipes that might be truly health-focused, but leave appeal at the door. Even with my deep passion for superfoods, I've been known to wrinkle my nose at greenish-grayish-brown smoothies that can only be greeted with, "This is good for me, right?" Rest assured, eating healthfully does not equate to drinking any shade of greenish-grayish-brown liquid—at least not in my book.

The superfood smoothies in this book are specifically designed to be incredibly delicious, but also excitingly energizing. Superfood recipes are about balancing flavor with function and, luckily, this is an easy goal to achieve with smoothies. So you'll better understand the basics, here are seven superfood smoothie principles: the golden rules for making the best, most beneficial smoothies ever. *Ever.* Blend by these basic principles and you will truly take your smoothies to the next level of healthy goodness.

1 Simple whole foods are the best ingredients of all.
Layering ingredients in your blender is one of the most exciting parts of making superfood smoothies—I love that the pitcher is transparent so you can see one fresh, whole ingredient after another forming layers of color and texture in a beautiful cornucopia, right before it is blended into yummy bliss. Superfood smoothies are whole-food dependent. They're made from nature's perfect alchemy of ingredients (like real fruits, vegetables, unrefined powders, nuts, and

seeds) and only use concentrated and processed ingredients to boost nutrition or bring flavors to their peak. Essentially, anything that didn't fall off a tree or get pulled from the ground should be considered an additive. It's not necessarily that these "additive" ingredients are bad—the ones used in this book certainly are not!—they just don't have nearly the same level of benefits as whole foods do. Always include whole fruits and vegetables first and foremost before resorting to concentrates or refined products.

2 **Every ingredient has a purpose.**

One of my favorite stand-up comedians, Louis C.K., dryly joked during one of his performances, "I've always eaten wrong. I didn't know food is a benefit to your body. I never looked at it that way. I always looked at food as another awful thing I'm about to do. . . . I never realized food is supposed to be good; it's supposed to make you feel good." For every one of us not born with a kale stem in his or her mouth, this self-revelation is part of the health journey and a profoundly exhilarating moment! Wheatgrass powder contains more than 70 types of vitamins and minerals in every spoonful. Hemp seeds contain essential fatty acids that are anti-inflammatory and help to nourish the brain, eyes, skin, and cardiovascular system. Maqui berries contain more anti-aging anthocyanin antioxidants than any other fruit yet discovered. When we change the way we think about food—as in, what it can do for

us—we become excitingly aware of our diet and are motivated to replace sub par "empty-calorie" foods with items that really offer something. What are your health objectives? More energy? Glowing skin? Disease protection? Superfoods are our friends, each offering compounded benefits for our mind and body. When you use them in smoothies, practice mindful blending and be conscious of every ingredient you include and how it benefits you. Just as the feeling of appreciation is often at the root of happiness, it can also make us feel healthy, as we are more tuned into the positive physical effects of our good choices.

It goes without saying that assessing the function of your smoothie ingredients will also increase your understanding and awareness of the other foods you consume in your life. Occasionally there will be times when less nutrient-dense ingredients will help round out taste, texture, and even color, but leaning on the best-choice options in a versatile diet is what creates lasting healthy change.

3 **More is not always better.**

I used to love carrot juice, drinking up to four servings a day (that's a full quart, for those of you doing the math), armed with the naive mantra "carrot juice is good for you." Indeed, it is. Yet within a few months, the palms of my hands and the bottoms of my feet had turned a noticeably deep orange, giving me the look of a self-tanning lotion repeat offender. I went to the doctor and learned that my odd new look was simply an accumulation of excess carotene, the orange antioxidant found in carrots. It was being stored harmlessly in my skin until my body could get around to processing it all. My doctor's prescription: Stop drinking so much carrot juice.

This third smoothie principle is for all my fellow overachievers out there—the ones who are always looking for that extra oomph, added edge, or next level. The nutrients in superfoods are much more condensed than in your average natural food, which is why we love them. Nonetheless, it's important to be respectful of these dense nutrition values. A half-teaspoon of camu powder offers almost 600% of the recommended daily allowance (RDA) of vitamin C, making it a great immunity-boosting addition to a smoothie. Tossing in a tablespoon of camu, however, would provide around 3500% RDA—far too much for the body to handle.

While the foods used in these recipes are not known to impose any dangers with overuse, overzealous tendencies can result in minor health problems like indigestion. Not to mention that gorging on foods for which you're paying a premium price becomes a waste of money if the body is not fully processing all the benefits. Even "tamer" foods, like everyday fruits, could produce huge sugar spikes if you were to include, say, six servings in one smoothie. This boils down to simple common sense: Be respectful of the "power" of superfoods (especially powders,

which are more dense); include them regularly but in moderate amounts. When in doubt, use the serving size on the package as a general guide for quantity.

4 **Nutrient density comes first.**
While in New York on a book tour, I became involved in a friendly yet heated debate with a woman after one of my talks. She insisted that calories were the be-all and end-all of understanding nutrition. While I agree that calories are a component of the equation, it is really the micronutrients, or rather, the amount of *micronutrients per calorie* that should be taken into account when assessing food choices.

As discussed in depth in my first book, *Superfood Kitchen*, nutrient density is the key to creating any superfood recipe, and it's especially important when making smoothies. Nutrient density refers to the ratio of micro-nutrients—vitamins, minerals, antioxidants, and phytochemicals—per calorie. The more micro-nutrients (or, as I call them, "benefits") each calorie of food has, the higher (better) the nutrient density of that food. Superfood smoothies are designed to be nutrient-dense—that is their primary purpose. Including superfoods, the most nutrient-dense foods of all, catapults these recipes to all-time highs in terms of nutrition. The remaining ingredients act to balance flavor and are the "best choice" non-superfoods intended to keep the benefit-to-calorie ratio as desirable as possible.

5 **Replace animal products with plant-based ingredients.**

Remember when the gym rat's daily go-to source for nutrition was a smoothie with raw eggs blended inside? Luckily for us, times have changed, and nutrition research has come a long way. While superfood smoothies aim to provide the most healthy benefits in a glassful, they also strive to do the least amount of bodily harm. Animal products of any kind—eggs, meat (which I trust you haven't put in a smoothie before, although I'm sure *someone* has), and all forms of dairy (milk, yogurt, ice cream, whey protein, etc.)—are not used in superfood smoothies because, while they may provide protein and some minerals, they also pose a very big health problem: acid. Animal products are some of the most acid-forming foods we consume, wreaking havoc on our bodies' pH balances and making us drastically more prone to disease (from minor to fatal) and accelerated aging. The macro- and micronutrients that animal products provide can be found in abundance in foods all across the plant kingdom, which offer all the benefits without the ugly health detriments. Going back to principle number two—remembering that every ingredient has a purpose—animal products do not help to achieve that. Lean on plants.

6 **Save the sugar for dessert.**

You might think this principle would be an obvious one, but take a quick look at many of

CREAMY INGREDIENT UPGRADES

Creamy flavor and texture is easily achieved with plant-based ingredients. To increase a smoothie's creaminess, blend in any of these foods:

- Avocado
- Banana
- Coconut
- Cooked grains (such as millet or barley)
- Cooked squash
- Dairy-free yogurt (sold at some health food stores)
- Mango
- Nut, rice, seed, or soy milks
- Rolled grains (such as oats or quinoa flakes)
- Soft tofu (organic, sprouted if available)
- Steamed root vegetables
- Whole raw seeds (used dry, or soaked in water for at least 1 hour for weaker blenders)
- Whole unsalted nuts (used dry, or soaked in water for at least 2 hours for weaker blenders)

the smoothie recipes out in the world and you'll have to agree that it's anything but! Superfood smoothies are a delicious sanctuary of healthy goodness, filled with natural foods to enhance health and wellness. They are not desserts, although many of them are certainly delicious enough to be desserts! With ingredients like fruit, fruit juice, and other healthier sweetening tricks, there is no need to include additional sugar in a smoothie. You can find the secrets on how to create sweeter smoothies without sugar on pages 10–12. If you eat sugar, save it for dessert and keep your smoothie clean.

It bears mentioning that chemical sweeteners of any kind (Splenda, aspartame, saccharine, and so on) are off the table as well. As most of them are known neurotoxins and carcinogens, these sweeteners should be kept out of smoothies . . . and, ideally, everything you consume.

7 **Superfood smoothies must taste good.**

Most of these principles are health-based, but I think happiness is also an important part of well-being, and a delicious smoothie means a happy drinker. With the right flavor combinations, smoothies can truly be like drinking a glass of Cloud 9—there's no need to wince while you gulp down murky, "healthy" sludge. Taking taste into consideration means you'll come to crave your daily boost via a superfood smoothie. In fact, you won't be able to go without it. Forget the temporary diet or sporadic "cleanse." A daily, tasty superfood smoothie paves the way to a healthy *lifestyle*. Start with deliciousness and your healthy endeavors and goals will be beyond easy . . . they will be absolutely irresistible.

SMOOTHIE BASICS

Smoothies are made following the most basic of recipes, but they do have a few general rules. A smoothie is typically composed of five components: a base (thickener), ice, liquid, flavoring agent, and sweetener. A superfood smoothie adds one additional layer to the mix: the all-important superfood boost, which we'll look at in depth starting on page 16.

CREATING THE BEST SMOOTHIE

Not all smoothies are created equal: The ingredients used for each of these components make or break the drink. For example, in theory, a smoothie could be made of ice cream (base and ice), milk (liquid), cake mix (flavoring agent), and sugar. Laugh at this recipe if you will, but I've seen it. Superfood smoothies aim to use the very best quality, nutritious ingredients in each layer to achieve the flavorful results that we crave. Creating something amazing is not just possible, it's *easy* when you have the knowledge and the healthy building blocks. Though the recipes in this book are designed to make your taste buds jump for joy (and give you the energy to jump even higher), you can also use this breakdown of top-tier smoothie ingredients as a guide to crafting your own healthy masterpieces.

Bases and Thickeners

The base of the smoothie is essentially the heart of the recipe. It brings the thickness, the texture, and some of the flavor. The possibilities are virtually endless: If you can blend it, it can be a suitable base! It's also an ideal layer to sneak in some extra servings of produce. The following foods work as delicious, nutritious bases:

Fatty fruits (such as avocados)
Frozen fruits
Frozen vegetables
Leafy greens
Nuts (unsalted)
Seeds (unsalted)
Some grains (such as rolled oats)
Steamed or roasted vegetables
Sweet fruits
Tofu

Ice

Whether a chilled, creamy drink or a frosty, spoonable mixture, smoothies taste best cold. Plain ice will do the job, but using different frozen ingredients is a trick that not only enhances the flavor of a smoothie, but adds nutrition as well, all while simplifying the recipe even further. Options include:

Ice
Flavored ice (see box on page 11)
Frozen fruits
Frozen vegetables

USING FROZEN VEGETABLES

Frozen vegetables are an underutilized secret to undetectably packing incredible amounts of vegetables into smoothies. Cold temperatures reduce our sensitivity to flavors, which is why, for example, a bite of fresh mango versus frozen mango tastes radically different. In the case of vegetables, this phenomenon works to our advantage, making vegetables remarkably easy to add into all varieties of blends. Additionally, using vegetables in a frozen form adds to the always desirable frosty texture . . . not to mention they can be stored infinitely longer than fresh ones. You can add virtually any frozen vegetable to a smoothie as long as it is unsalted and unflavored. Some top frozen vegetables to use in smoothies include:

- Broccoli
- Brussels sprouts
- Cauliflower
- Chopped spinach
- Peas

Liquids

Of course, it wouldn't be a smoothie if it was just a collection of solid foods! Liquid is essential for blending ingredients into a smooth mixture, and can also help to balance out flavor. Depending on your personal preference and dietary objectives, you can use something as simple as water or as rich as coconut milk. The most important rule: Make sure your liquid of choice is cold from the start—no one likes a lukewarm smoothie.

By the way, if you don't make nondairy milks yourself at home (page 184 shows you how) and use store-bought brands instead, always make sure you choose unsweetened varieties—in other words, read those labels! Starting with unsweetened products gives you 100% control of how—and how much—your smoothie is sweetened, thereby avoiding excess hidden sugars that can sneak into smoothies made with even the best intentions. In making the healthiest recipes, it's all about control. Choose from:

Coconut water
Fruit juice
Kombucha or keifer (fermented drinks)
Nut and seed milks
    (store-bought or homemade)
Prepared tea (cooled)
Rice milk
Soy milk*
Vegetable juice
Water

Flavorings

Adding natural flavoring agents can help take a decent-tasting smoothie into crave-worthy, wow-factor deliciousness. Using flavorings can also help smooth over and hide any "rough patches" in flavor (from broccoli or chlorella [algae] powder, for example). Don't be afraid to get creative with some of the natural extracts in the baking aisle. These important ingredients may not add much nutrition, but they do help boost nutrient density by helping to cut unnecessary calories traditionally contributed by high-flavor, high-calorie foods, all while leaving your taste buds wanting more of the good stuff. Consider using these ingredients:

Extracts (such as almond, mint, etc.)**
Freeze-dried fruit powder**
Fresh citrus zest
Fresh herbs (such as mint, basil,
    rosemary, etc.)
Fresh lemon juice
Fresh lime juice
Freshly ground vanilla bean
    or vanilla extract
Ground spices (such as cinnamon, nutmeg,
    cardamom, etc.)
Lucuma powder**
Mesquite powder**

---

* Note that soy milk is not used as an ingredient in this book. I believe soy milk is fine to consume on occasion (as long as it's organic), but soy is an overused ingredient in the modern diet, and can potentially cause health imbalances or even allergies if overconsumption occurs. There are so many other wonderful options for nondairy "milks" that are worthy of rotation that I suggest using soymilk sparingly in smoothies, if at all.

** These ingredients are not needed for any recipes in this book, but can add wonderful flavor variety. A few drops of almond extract, for example, turns a creamy smoothie into a dessert-like experience, and low-glycemic mesquite powder (available in health food stores and online) naturally sweetens with a carob-meets-caramel flavor.

LOVING LUCUMA IN SMOOTHIES

Although it contains some vitamins (particularly the Bs), carotene antioxidants, and a few minerals, lucuma doesn't quite earn a *superfood* star. Nonetheless, it is a star ingredient in smoothies. A South American fruit that looks like an avocado on the outside, with a rich orange interior, lucuma tastes like a cross between a mango and a sweet potato. It is an exceptionally popular dessert fruit in South America, most often used to flavor ice cream. Unsurprisingly, lucuma also makes a brilliant smoothie addition, lending a sweet, slightly fruity, slightly creamy flavor, with notes of vanilla and caramel. Sold in North America in a powdered form, lucuma may seem like an unnecessarily gourmet addition to smoothies, but its low-sugar sweetness helps cut down sugar content while catapulting flavor. It can sometimes be hard to find lucuma powder, even in health food stores, so I recommend ordering it online (see page 187 for information on sources).

Sweeteners

Sweeteners are, perhaps, the second most important consideration in creating a truly healthy smoothie (superfoods being the first). Just as salt brings out the flavors in savory foods, sweeteners help extract and heighten the flavors in smoothies. I believe that properly sweetening smoothies is an absolute must. It's the difference between making a good-for-you smoothie that is drinkable but forgettable and one that is so delicious you can't put it down—and can't wait to incorporate it into your lifestyle.

If you're into pleasing the palette, using sweeteners properly can make or break a smoothie. However, like salt, the perfect amount of "sweet" is very much an individual preference. You'll notice that in each recipe in this book, I recommend that you test the blend first, and then use "sweetener, to taste." Some recipes will be perfect as is; others may need a slight extra edge, so add a bit more sweetener.

Of course, when we talk about sweeteners, we're not talking about adding a spoonful of sugar to make the medicine go down. Instead, we're calling on the abundance of healthier alternative sweeteners—our "best choice" sweeteners—which offer more benefits than some of their more concentrated or processed counterparts. Without getting into the nuances of nutrition, it's important to remember that sweeteners of any kind are to always be used with care—even the best-choice ones. I remember a woman saying to me once while in a supermarket line: "I love smoothies. I put in tons of superfoods, like fruit and agave nectar." To clear up any potential confusion: Sweeteners are not superfoods. They're not even really health foods. But, again, if using a half-tablespoon of a "best choice" sweetener like agave nectar is the difference between making a smoothie that you may drink half of and a

MAKING FLAVORED ICE

Using flavored ice is one of the true secrets to raising the bar on smoothies. While it may seem like an unnecessary step, flavored ice adds an extra dimension of flavor, and can help to mimic the effect of adding ice cream or sherbet to a smoothie. The technique is as simple as it is versatile: Pour a beverage such as juice or almond milk into ice cube trays and freeze until solid. For best results, use a flexible silicone tray with a lid, which keeps the flavors fresh and allows the ice cubes to be easily removed (see the Resource Guide on page 187 for brand suggestions).

Though you can freeze virtually any beverage into an ice, to keep things simple, three different types of flavored ice are called for in this book. Here's how to make them:

Coconut Ice: Freeze pure coconut water in ice cube trays until solid. (A favorite for adding flavor.)

Almond Ice: Freeze unsweetened almond milk in ice cube trays until solid.

Green Tea Ice: Freeze prepared unsweetened green tea in ice cube trays until solid.

If you experiment with other types of flavored ice, keep in mind that the higher the sugar content (as in high-sugar fruit juices) and/or fat content (as in canned coconut milk), the softer the ice will be and the faster it will melt. This is one reason I recommend unsweetened liquids, especially teas, for making ice. All flavored ices will melt slightly more quickly than pure ice, so feel free to add additional ice if needed to achieve the desired texture.

Properly covered, flavored ices will keep indefinitely in the freezer, making them easy to make in large quantities and have on hand as needed. Different trays vary in yield, but most ice trays will produce about 2–3 cups of ice.

smoothie that you can't put down, I suggest going with the choice that will create a happy habit!

My personal favorite smoothie sweetener is stevia extract. Sold in both powdered and liquid forms, stevia is made from a garden herb that is profoundly sweet to the taste buds. Stevia has no calories, no carbohydrates, no sugar, and no effect on blood sugar, plus it has none of the health-compromising side effects that artificial sugar substitutes have. It's a brilliant tool in

the healthy kitchen, and I use it all the time to lightly boost the flavor of my smoothies.

Stevia's one downside is that it is a very distinct type of "sweet." A highly concentrated extract, stevia acts similarly to some of its artificial competition, providing a flat, almost sharp, sweetness. It is very difficult to use successfully in recipes that are baked or cooked, as its potency is difficult to control in situations where it is unable to be added to taste. It also lacks the "rounded" flavor of other sugary options if used alone. However, stevia is ideal for recipes like smoothies that already have some natural sweetness and just need an extra boost. While a little stevia can make flavors sing, using too much will create a distinct bitter aftertaste. Since everybody's palate is different, some people are more sensitive to this bitterness than others, adamantly proclaiming how much they *don't* like stevia. Perhaps you're one of these people; if so, I plead you to give stevia one more try. If you can learn to like the taste, it really is a magic wand that can create the sweetness you crave while cheating calories and sugar like nothing else can. Nine times out of ten, people who claim to "hate stevia" have simply used too much in a recipe—an easy accident because of stevia's über-sweet concentration. Therefore, I highly recommend that both new stevia users and stevia skeptics alike try it out in liquid form. It comes in a vial, so you add just one drop at a time, allowing you to taste-test to perfection.

The list below outlines a few of my favorite smoothie sweeteners, in order of "best choice." With few exceptions, however, I usually use stevia. Smoothies seem to be what this crazy herb was born to sweeten, and it keeps the recipe's nutrient density at its peak. You can easily pick a favorite sweetener or two to use for all your smoothies.

WHAT TO LEAVE OUT

If you're making the investment of putting super-foods into your blender, don't undermine your efforts by adding counterproductive ingredients. Though sometimes found in commercial smoothie blends, these foods have a low nutrient density with potentially negative health consequences, so avoid the following whenever possible:

- Cane sugar and cane juice (or products containing it)
- Corn syrup
- Dairy (including milk, yogurt, and ice cream)
- Eggs
- Food coloring
- Isolated soy protein
- Protein powders that include any of these ingredients
- Pudding or cake mixes
- Whey protein

Agave nectar
Date syrup
Dates
Jerusalem artichoke syrup (very pricy, but low on the glycemic index)
Maple syrup
Stevia (liquid or powder)
Xylitol (use varieties not derived from corn)
Yacon syrup (expensive, but beneficial)

SUPERFOOD SMOOTHIE ESSENTIALS

To say superfoods are important is an understatement. As I discuss at length in my first book, *Superfood Kitchen*, incorporating superfoods in our diet is more essential than ever before. The abundance of empty calories found in the standard American diet has left us in a dire state, desperately trying deal with all-time high rates of obesity, heart disease, diabetes, and cancer. Coupled with nutrient loss in crops thanks to factory farming, even the freshest plant-based diets are deprived of the micronutrients we need. And then along come superfoods, providing just the nutritional sustenance we've been looking for.

Packed with more vitamins, minerals, antioxidants, and phytochemicals—and thus, overall benefits—than any other foods on the planet, superfoods clearly live up to their name as our little nutritional superheroes. Instead of taxing our bodies with toxins, calories, and difficult-to-digest substances, superfoods offer only the vital good stuff; they're a distilled way of eating healthily, if you will. Think of it like panning for gold—where "panning" a normal food may result in mostly silt with a few gold flakes sprinkled in (if you're lucky), the superfood pan is gleaming all over with glittery flakes and gold nuggets, with very little dirt to filter out. Our bodies feel like they've struck it rich when fueled with superfoods, and in turn reward us with

the health goals we crave: a body in optimum shape, energy to perform our best (mentally and physically), and a preventative armor against even the most serious diseases that plague our society. Just from eating delicious food. Not such a bad deal, is it? It's just a matter of doing it, and smoothies take out all the stress of "how." Just blend 'em!

THE "SUPER 15"

Although nature has provided us with a wealth of superfoods to choose from, let's face it—most of us don't have the budget, the kitchen space, or even just the mental space to take on the entire world's collection of superfoods. So, for the purpose of the recipes in this book, I've selected the "Super 15" of superfoods—the top core superfoods for holistic well-being that we'll incorporate into smoothies in the recipe section. Each superfood on the list has earned its spot by being a valuable addition to enhancing broad-spectrum health, readily available in health food stores or online, palatable and blender-friendly, and cost-effective in terms of nutrients per serving and per dollar.

If these items are new to your kitchen, don't worry! There's no need to run to the health food store and stock up on every ingredient right away. Rather, pick a new superfood every week or so to feature in your blender, and make one of the fabulous recipes on the following pages based on what's in your pantry. For the longest time

I was exclusively a cacao, maca, and goji girl, before finally branching out and incorporating (with great success, I should add) other natural treasures. Since every superfood has its own unique set of benefits, becoming more versatile in your superfoods can only enhance overall well being. Nonetheless, I recognize that everyone needs to start somewhere, so don't be afraid to start small . . . or wherever you're comfortable. Every superfood you incorporate can only enhance, not hurt.

Acai Berries

Though acai's popularity in North America is growing at a rapid pace, it is still considered a relatively exotic food. Meanwhile, in South America, acai is tremendously common—practically a staple, especially in beach communities. A small berry that grows on a type of tall palm tree, acai has a dark blue-purple hue, a mild berry flavor, and is slightly oily and creamy in a very pleasant way. Its delicate flavor can be easily overwhelmed by other ingredients, but is brought out in smoothies with bananas, creamy nut milks (including coconut milk), other berries, and dates. Acai strikes a particularly nice balance with chocolate, but it rarely matches well with vegetables or citrus. With its luscious taste and texture, acai almost seems as if it was created specifically to go in smoothies. In fact, acai drinks are the preferred preparation method in the berry's indigenous regions.

Buying: Health food and conventional grocery store shelves alike are increasingly shelving various acai products. For the purpose of smoothies, the most important qualities to look for in acai are purity and simplicity. This means any acai product with added sweeteners is not recommended.* Remember our principle: using pure ingredients gives you complete control over the contents of your smoothie, which allows you to optimize flavor and health benefits. My go-to form of acai is freeze-dried powder (pictured above). I like this form for several reasons: It's portable (great for travel), is much less perishable than juice (keep it in the freezer for an even longer

---

* You will often see the addition of citric acid to acai products—this is simply vitamin C added to help preserve acai's fats, which are very delicate and will quickly go rancid on the shelf without some protection. Citric acid is a very natural, even beneficial, preservative, and nothing to worry about in small amounts.

shelf life—the powder will not solidify), and is hyper-concentrated and completely unadulterated. Other good forms include pure acai juice with no sugars added and sugar-free acai pulp "smoothie packs," found in the frozen section of some health food stores. For the recipes in this book you'll only need the freeze-dried powder, but feel free to experiment with other forms.

Benefits: Acai is most celebrated for its high levels of antioxidants, which make it exceptional at fighting free radicals and aging and at promoting longevity. Rich in minerals, vitamins, and amino acids, acai is a "fatty" fruit that also contains EFAs (essential fatty acids) including omega-3, 6, and 9, as well as heart-healthy monosaturated fats. Acai has the added benefit of being low in sugar.

Serving Size: 1 tablespoon freeze-dried acai powder.

Substitutes: There's nothing quite like the flavor of acai, which is part of the reason it is becoming so popular here in North America. However, if health benefits are the primary criterion, maqui powder (discussed on pages 28–29) can be used in place of acai. In general, use about 1 teaspoon maqui berry powder to 1 tablespoon acai powder since maqui is more highly concentrated.

Algae

This primeval superfood is among the oldest life-forms on earth, and also one of the most nutrient-dense. A warning, however: Edible algae has a prominent flavor, which may be difficult to overcome. Some people don't mind the flavor at all, while others are more sensitive to it. Do the best you can with this superfood—it's worth its weight in gold in terms of detoxifying benefits, so even the tiniest pinch is better than nothing at all.

In general, algae work best when used in very small amounts in smoothies featuring strong flavors such as chocolate, apple, or lemon to help balance the taste of "ocean." Another trick is to keep the smoothie very cold and icy, which naturally reduces flavor sensitivity in the taste buds. Drinking the blend while very fresh also helps; the longer the smoothie is allowed to sit, the more the algae flavor will be amplified.

Varieties: The most commonly available green and blue-green algae are chlorella and spirulina, respectively. I recommend chlorella over spirulina as it has substantially more chlorophyll, but both are phenomenally beneficial.

Buying: Look in the supplements section in health or natural food stores (or online). Source is important, because algae acts as a microfilter of the water in which it's grown, so purchase brands that provide purity testing (there is no organic certification when it comes to algae). Only buy chlorella when the package says it is a "cracked wall" variety; this ensures that it is digestible.

Benefits: Both spirulina and chlorella are largely made up of protein (amino acids), and offer staggering quantities of micronutrients, containing as many as 40 types of minerals (they're especially high in iron), and incredible stores of vitamin A, vitamin K, vitamin D (there's a whopping 240% RDA in just 5 grams of chlorella), and the B vitamins. With as much as 1–2% of its weight composed of pure chlorophyll, this superfood is perhaps the most potent cleansing food found in nature, and is well known to be particularly helpful in the elimination of heavy metals and toxins.

Serving Size: ½–1 teaspoon a day. If you are new to using algae, start with half a serving; in some cases it can trigger too strong of a cleansing reaction.

Substitutes: Use a dried greens powder (like wheatgrass powder or your favorite blend), a liquid chlorophyll concentrate, or omit entirely.

Cacao

It may be wrong to pick favorites, but cacao often wins the hearts of even the most experienced superfood adventurers. Its popularity is understandable: The raw form of chocolate, cacao is a not just a typical superfood, but a phenomenal one. Adding it to smoothies is a thrill—a chocolate, anti-aging, energizing, health-giving, and did I mention *chocolate* smoothie? You bet! Cacao can be included in blends to make dessert-like smoothies, imparting its alluring flavor wherever it goes. It works best with nut milks and creamy ingredients like avocados and bananas, but can be used with fruits like berries, and even mild green vegetables such as spinach. It does not combine particularly well with most tropical and citrus fruits (orange is an exception).

Varieties: Though there are many sub-species of cacao, these are minute technicalities. When purchasing cacao, it is more important to make sure it is either fair-trade certified or from a company that supports fair-trade practices.

Buying: The two forms of cacao that work best for smoothies are cacao powder (the most nutrient-dense form of cacao) and cacao nibs. Cacao powder offers a stronger flavor and will blend effortlessly into a smooth drink, while cacao nibs will usually retain a small, fun element of crunchiness, even after blending. Note that cocoa powder is a different product: It is the roasted form of cacao and, while still beneficial, it does not provide the same level of nutrients, especially antioxidants.

Benefits: There are an incredible number of benefits to cacao. First, it is among the most mineral-rich superfoods, containing calcium and iron, and earns the title of the highest magnesium food. It also is considered to be energizing and mood-enhancing due to its effects as a mild central nervous system stimulant, and increases the serotonin levels in the brain (serotonin is the feel-good chemical that helps support a positive outlook, emotional health, restful sleep, and more). Cacao is off the charts in its levels of antioxidants, too: With an ORAC (Oxygen Radical Absorbance Capacity, the unit used to measure antioxidants) of 95,000 per 100 grams of cacao powder, it's almost double the score of antioxidant-rich acai powder. Amazing! Rich in polyphenols that help reduce bad cholesterol and support heart health, cacao can even help protect the skin against inflammation. The question becomes: Is there anything cacao can't do?

Serving Size: 2½ tablespoons cacao powder, 2 tablespoons cacao nibs.

Substitutes: Use pure, organic, fair-trade cocoa powder in place of cacao powder (be sure there are no additives). Note that the amount of anti-oxidants found in cocoa is significantly less than that in cacao.

Camu Berries

I think of camu berries as the South American cranberry: They look similar (although camu is lighter in color), grow in floodplains, and are quite tart. With its pale brown color and bitter taste, camu berry powder is a bit of an ugly duckling in the world of superfood powders, but its benefits are so concentrated that using literally just a pinch will enhance a smoothie with more vitamin C than taking a pill. Camu berry powder is a superfood I strongly suggest investing in—even the smallest bag lasts for ages. And because you're using a teaspoon at a time (or a quarter of that!), you can add it into virtually anything. At my house, I boost almost every smoothie I make with camu—it's in the "why not?" category of superfoods.

Buying: If you happen to be in South America, you can get camu berries fresh, or even in a juice! For the rest of us, camu berry powder is the way to go. It's easy to store and use; be sure it is 100% organic.

Benefits: Camu berries are nature's number-one source of vitamin C: A single teaspoon contains almost 1200% RDA! This makes camu berries a very effective immunity-boosting superfood, excellent for skin and beauty, and a great anti-inflammatory, anti-viral, anti-bacterial, and anti-fungal agent.

Serving Size: ½ teaspoon pure camu berry powder.

Substitutes: Camu berry powder is used solely for its vitamin C benefit. So little of it is used in recipes, however, that if you don't have it, it may be easiest to skip a replacement altogether. If you want that extra vitamin C, however, other concentrated sources include superfoods like cupacu and rose hips (neither are required for the recipes in this book and thus not discussed), citrus fruits, and cranberries.

Chia Seeds

Blink and you may miss them—smaller than sesame seeds, chia seeds are one of the tiniest edible seeds around. Indigenous to Central America, this traditional Incan food has been viewed as a staple energy food for centuries. Chia is finally getting a renewed lease on popularity, especially among athletes, health practitioners, and dieters. Almost flavorless, chia is an absolute breeze to add to smoothies—it goes with almost anything you can dream up.

Outside of its health benefits [*] (discussed shortly), chia has one additional, very unique property that makes it a particularly valuable superfood to use in smoothies: mucilage. Mucilage is a compound found in plants that helps them to retain water, and chia seeds happen to contain

MAKING CHIA GEL

A smart way to increase thickness, lower calories, and boost the superfood content of smoothies is to add chia gel. When chia seed is combined with liquid, it absorbs the surrounding water to form a jellylike substance, fondly known by many as "chia gel." The texture of these little gel "balls" feels fun sliding around on your tongue, but over-blending will ruin the effect. For this reason, add chia gel after the smoothie is already blended, then blend very briefly once more just to mix it.

TO MAKE THE GEL:

Mix together 2 cups of water with 4 tablespoons chia seeds. Let stand for 15 minutes. Mix again, then let stand for 15 minutes longer to allow the seeds to swell to maximum capacity. Refrigerated, chia gel will last for one week. Makes 2¼ cups.

Virtually flavorless, the consistency of chia gel can be altered by changing the quantity of seeds used (add more for a thicker gel or fewer for a thinner texture). For best results, use a mason jar or sealable container to shake the chia and water vigorously together instead of stirring by hand. Not mixing the seeds well enough will result in the formation of undesirable, chewy, and dense chia "clumps." Plus, using a sealable jar means your chia gel will already be prepared for easy storage in the refrigerator.

FLAVORED VARIATIONS:

Though not used in the recipes in this book, chia seeds can also be soaked in various liquids to create different flavors of chia gel. Try beverages like apple juice, grape juice, or kombucha to create fun variations of your favorite smoothie recipes.

an exorbitant amount of it. In fact, chia seeds are able to retain around 8 to 9 times their weight in water when left to soak for just 15 minutes. Like some odd science experiment, they swell up and form a jellylike protective layer around themselves, resembling a miniature ball of tapioca. Because of this trait, chia seeds make an excellent thickening agent for smoothies without adding significant calories. And they're fully digestible just putting them in the blender as is, meaning you don't need to grind the seeds into a

powder to access the benefits. Either make a chia gel beforehand (see above for instructions) and mix it in your smoothie immediately, or add dry chia seeds to your blend and allow it to chill for about half an hour to allow the chia seeds to work their "gelling" magic. Because of its lack of flavor, chia is a star superfood to work with, open to so many smoothie possibilities.

Varieties: There are two varieties of chia seeds found on the market today: brown chia, which actually varies in color from dark brown to gray to white, and white chia, which is considered an heirloom variety. They are nearly identical in their nutritional and flavor profiles—use whichever you prefer.

Buying: You'll most commonly come across plain chia seeds, but there are also ground chia powders and even sprouted chia powders. All are wonderful superfood products and may be used interchangeably. Chia seeds are better if you'd like to experience the texture of chia gel; chia powder is preferable if you'd rather the chia be undetectable in your smoothie.

Benefits: Chia is a true powerhouse of nutrition, best known for its healthy fats, high fiber content, and antioxidants. But perhaps its attributes are best appreciated by how it compares to other foods. In addition to a slew of minerals and protein, ounce-for-ounce chia contains eight times more omega-3s than salmon, five times more calcium than milk, three times more iron than spinach, and three times more antioxidants than blueberries. Its magic combination of easily digestible high nutrition, low calories, and incredible satiation effects are what make it such a dynamic food for weight loss, sustainable energy, and longevity.

Serving Size: 2 tablespoons chia seeds or 1½ tablespoons chia powder.

Substitutes: Ground flaxseeds may be used in the place of chia seeds in a 1:1 ratio. Although ground flaxseeds will help to thicken smoothies, they will not have the same texture as a true chia gel (no mini tapioca balls, just jellylike goo).

Chlorophyll-rich Superfoods

Chlorophyll is the pigment in plants that makes them appear green—the molecules that harvest solar energy and, via photosynthesis, convert it into energy. This energy is transferred to us when we consume it, making green vegetables the core secret to staying young and vibrant. I don't want to say that you can *never* have too many greens, but let's just say you'd have to try really, really hard to overdo it. For those of us who are looking to get more, smoothies are an ideal vessel for sneaking in extra greens without having to exclusively live on salads or, frankly, even taste them at all. "Green" smoothies are gaining a strong following as a convincing and convenient way to get more of this important food group in your diet, and there is an entire section of this book, beginning on page 76 devoted to just this color of the smoothie movement. They may be green, but they taste incredibly good!

Varieties: In addition to the fresh leafy greens found in the produce section (from lettuce to kale to watercress) and deep green vegetables (like broccoli or cucumber with the skin), outstanding concentrations of nutrients can be found in grasses (like wheatgrass or barley grass) and sprouts (like mild-tasting sunflower or clover sprouts).

Buying: Look for crisp, unwilted greens. Fresh young greens will be the least fibrous and have the most delicate flavor. Any slimy leaves should be tossed immediately, as they can harbor bacteria. Extra-convenient "greens" powders are now readily available as well, from pure freeze-dried wheatgrass powder (a personal favorite), to blends that may contain as many as twenty types of green vegetables. Each powder variety tastes a little different, so use according to taste, and watch for uncertain fillers on the ingredient lists. Frozen green vegetables also make ideal additions to smoothies (see page 8), and are great for long-term storage. For a flavorless chlorophyll shot, try a chlorophyll concentrate, usually made from distilled alfalfa or nettles. Lastly, fresh, green, pure vegetable juice is wonderful. Although it's not included in the recipes in this book due to lack of widespread availability, it's an ideal addition to any fruit-based smoothie.

Benefits: Containing vast amounts of vitamins and minerals, greens are in many ways nature's multivitamin. They are often especially high in vitamin C, vitamin E, beta carotene, folic acid, iron, and potassium, and are one of the best sources of calcium, to name just a few of the nutritional benefits. The abundance of anti-oxidizing chlorophyll helps detoxify and cleanse the body, promotes circulation and overall energy, and balances out the body's pH, which is often in need of correction due to our primarily acid-forming diets. One last, often forgotten, benefit of greens is their protein content. Collectively covering all the essential amino acids, many greens contain an exceptional amount of protein in relation to their low calories; for example, broccoli and spinach each provide around 5 grams of protein per cup.

Serving Size: 1 (packed) cup for leafy greens, ½ cup sprouts, ½–1 teaspoon wheatgrass or barley grass powder. Use greens powders as directed on their package.

Substitutes: A serving of powder can often be substituted for a serving of fresh, and vice versa. Most greens can easily be swapped for one another, but note that some are more potent in their "green" flavor than others. (The same goes for greens powders—some have virtually no flavor, while others are like a bite of broccoli. See the Resource Guide on page 187 for recommendations.) A cup of romaine lettuce, for example, will have almost no flavor in a smoothie, while a cup of kale will be more noticeable. For the mildest green flavor possible, use wheatgrass powder; for a fresh but almost undetectable addition, use baby spinach.

Flaxseed

Part of the human diet for 7,000 years, these small, tough, glossy seeds have a mild, nutty flavor that drops to the background of most blended drinks when used in small quantities. Full of important functions yet surprisingly inexpensive, flaxseeds are a great "starter" superfood for anyone looking to boost a blender drink on the dime. To access the benefits of flax, it must be ground into a powder prior to consuming it, otherwise the seeds will pass through the body undigested. Depending on the blender you have, adding whole flaxseeds to the blender may be all you need to do. But if you have questionable faith in your machine, add pre-ground flax to your recipe (all the recipes in this book call for flax in this form). You can either buy it already in powder form or freshly grind the whole seeds in a coffee or spice grinder.

Varieties: Flax is readily available in two varieties: brown flax and golden flax. Containing very similar nutritional indexes, either or both can be used in smoothies.

Buying: If you're looking to buy flax powder, I recommend getting the best variety on the market: sprouted flax powder, which actually adds nutritional value to the seed through the natural process of sprouting. You can also purchase regular flax powder, but it is much more cost-effective to buy whole flaxseeds (look for them in bulk) and grind them in a spice or coffee grinder on an as-needed basis. The delicate oils of flaxseeds break down easily, so store any unused seeds or powder in the refrigerator or freezer.

Benefits: Flaxseed is one of the best sources of essential fatty acids, which help to keep the brain healthy, act as anti-inflammatory agents, and are excellent for heart and joint health. Overflowing with vitamin E, flax is an excellent boost for healthy skin. It is also rich in compounds called lignans, which help to balance hormone levels, making flax a great anti-PMS food. Plus, at about 30% dietary fiber, flax is excellent for colon health.

Serving Size: 2 tablespoons whole flaxseed or 1½ tablespoons ground flax powder (sprouted or regular).

Substitutes: Chia seeds and chia seed powder can be used at a 1:1 ratio to flax.

Goji Berries

Goji berries have been used in Chinese medicine for thousands of years, and are often referred to as the "longevity fruit." Their taste is reminiscent of a raisin married with a cranberry—mostly sweet, with a slight tartness. Traditionally, goji berries have been used in beverages—specifically, in teas—and their mild flavor makes them an exceptionally easy superfood addition, meshing well with anything from fruits to vegetables to more rich ingredients like chocolate and nuts. Some fruits, like citrus and mango, enhance the goji's flavor, but for anyone interested primarily in the benefits, the truth is, a few spoonfuls of goji berries can be added to virtually any smoothie blend for a boost. Because it is typically sold and used in dried form (pictured to the right), goji's already high nutrient density is even further condensed and amplified; a loose handful of goji berries is all that is really needed to enjoy a serving.

Buying: Dried goji berries are the most readily available form. Always be sure to buy certified organic goji berries (they can be subjected to high levels of pesticides when grown conventionally), and never buy berries that have sugar or preservatives added. Goji berry powder, pasteurized goji juice, and frozen goji berries are also available in some health food stores—all are great additions to smoothies, as well. For the purpose of the

recipes in this book, we will be exclusively using dried goji berries for their wide accessibility and flavor. When purchasing dried goji berries, look for ones that have a strong reddish color—never buy brown ones. Good-quality berries will have a slight chew and should not be crunchy, which means they either were overly dried or are old. If buying in bags, always check the "best by" date to make sure your goji berries are not past their prime.

Benefits: Goji berries are amazingly balanced, containing all of the major macronutrients (complete protein, fat, and carbohydrate) and over twenty vitamins and minerals. With ever-increasing amounts of research being done on this superfood, goji berries have been shown in clinical trials to support vision (including macular degeneration and cataracts), aid the immune system, improve memory (including fighting against Alzheimer's disease), and act as a potent anti-carcinogen.

Serving Size: 3 tablespoons dried goji berries, or 1 ounce by weight.

Substitutes: Dried goji berries may be used interchangeably with different forms of goji (powder, juice, or frozen) on a serving-for-serving basis. Although not as beneficial, dried mulberries or even raisins can be used as a full substitute for goji berries in a 1:1 ratio.

Hemp Seeds

A sustainable, versatile crop in the same botanical family as mulberries, hemp seeds are harvested from the *Cannabis sativa* plant, an industrial relative of marijuana (without the THC). Small and golden, with a tiny, green, chlorophyll-filled filament on the inside, hemp seeds taste similar to sunflower seeds and, when added to smoothies, lend an extra creamy note. Simply blending water and hemp seeds together (use about 3 tablespoons of seeds per cup of water) will make a delicate hemp "milk"—which is exactly what happens when incorporating them into a smoothie.

Because they pack in so much plant-based protein, hemp seeds are also sold as a refined powder that concentrates this benefit. Called simply "hemp protein powder" or sometimes just "hemp powder," these products vary widely—some will be gritty and earthy and will only work when masked inside of very creamy or very icy smoothies. Others are more refined and have a nutty flavor, making them easier to use. (See the Resource Guide on page 187 for the hemp protein powder that I like to use, which is the smoothest I've found.) Whether using hemp protein powder or hemp seeds, the smoothies that work best with these ingredients are ones that contain other creamy elements, such as nuts, bananas, and cacao. Fruit will occasionally work with hemp seeds, as long as a minimal amount of hemp is used.

Varieties: Edible hemp is the only kind of hemp sold at the grocery store—I promise you won't accidently buy marijuana seeds.

Buying: When buying hemp seeds to use in smoothies, make sure that they are pre-shelled, raw, and unsalted. When buying hemp protein powder, look for a plain powder without any additives. Although supporting organic farms is always important, it's nice to know that hemp is inherently a very hardy crop, and needs little to no pesticides to grow.

Benefits: Hemp seeds are one of the best sources of protein on the planet, and include all eight essential amino acids. Hemp is very easily digestible, and closer to the alkaline end of the pH scale than almost any other solid protein source except for greens. Hemp protein powders range in concentration from around 15 to 21 grams of protein per 3 tablespoons; hemp seeds have about 5 grams per 2 tablespoons. Hemp seeds are also a wonderful source of essential fatty acids, providing heart- and skin-healthy omega-3s in abundance, as well as GLA (gamma-linolenic acid), which can help balance hormones. Using more hemp is a great way to add additional minerals into smoothies, as well, especially iron, magnesium, and zinc.

Serving Size: 3 tablespoons for hemp seeds, 2–3 tablespoons for hemp protein powder.

Substitutes: Though not as beneficial, sunflower seeds may be used in place of hemp seeds for a similar flavor effect. Rice protein powder or your favorite protein powder blend can be used in place of plain hemp protein powder, though do note that many blended brands are flavored, which will affect the overall taste of the recipe.

Maca

A thick, radish-like root that's related to the mustard family, maca is native to the remote peaks of the Peruvian Andes in the Puna region of southern Peru, the highest altitude of any farming region in the world. Maca is farmed by Andean Indians in the unusual areas it seems to prefer: largely barren and rocky landscapes with intense sun, consistent fierce winds, and drastic daily temperature fluctuations that often drop to below-freezing temperatures at sunset. Clearly, maca is an incredibly strong and resilient plant: Not only does it manage to battle extreme elements, but it actually thrives in them.

In North America, maca is typically sold in powdered form, which offers a unique malty, earthy flavor that varies from butterscotch- to radish-like, depending on the flavors of the foods it's accompanying. It is a very potent ingredient that will rarely go unnoticed. Best used in creamy smoothies with nut or seed bases, it also pairs well with very sweet fruits like bananas and dates. Most fruits, however, are not compatible with maca's flavor, and it can be very disruptive to the flavor of vegetable blends as well. There is little gray area between maca's ability to taste either delicious or bizarre.

Varieties: Maca comes in different colors: red, yellow, purple, and black. Some believe that each color variety has a slightly different affect on the body; however, there is very limited scientific evidence to support this at this time. More important than the color is choosing a high-quality, organic maca powder (in fact, most maca brands will not mention the color at all). My maca recommendation in the Resource Guide on page 187 is a blend of several different colors of organic Peruvian maca to ensure, potentially, the largest spectrum of benefits.

Buying: When purchasing maca, there are three forms to choose from. The first is a raw maca powder, which is simply whole maca root that has been sun-dried and ground at low temperatures into a fine, caramel-colored powder. This is the purest form, and the most common outside of its immediate growing regions. The second type is a gelatinized powder (a fancy way of saying maca concentrate) that is more potent than the raw powder, as the maca's starchy fiber—which many people find difficult to digest—has been removed. Due to its potency, I prefer using maca in this form, but the two powders have little difference in flavor. Lastly, maca tinctures and maca capsules exist as well, but these are not advised for those looking to utilize maca as a food product.

Benefits: Maca is a true energy food. To understand the many benefits of maca, we must recognize its role as a powerful adaptogen, helping us balance stress and maintain a state of equilibrium. Research shows maca's adaptogenic compounds directly support the adrenal glands to help balance hormones and enhance energy without being a stimulant. Both the endocrine system, which transports oxygen throughout the blood and promotes healthy neurotransmitter production, and the thyroid, which effects our bodies' strength and stamina, benefit from this superfood. Maca has been used to improve everything from chronic fatigue to anemia to lack of libido; it can help decrease anxiety and stress; and it has long had a reputation for enhancing fertility. It is high in a wide spectrum of essential minerals, including iron, iodine, calcium, magnesium, phosphorus, potassium, zinc, selenium, and more, and contains healthy doses of several vitamins, such as vitamins B1, B2, C, and E. Packed with amino acids, maca is a notable source of an array of plant sterols, which enhance the immune system and have been shown to be helpful in lowering cholesterol. It helps to normalize hormones like testosterone, progesterone, and estrogen—and has been shown to increase libido by 180%! Interestingly, maca seems to be able to retain much of its nutrition even after years of storage, unlike most plants, which lose their nutritional integrity a brief period of time after harvest. In many ways, maca truly is the "survival plant."

Serving Size: Most people benefit from taking around 1 tablespoon of maca powder a day, but more or less can be taken as needed. If you've never used maca before, start out with just a teaspoon a day, and build upward as you see fit. Maca is a very powerful superfood, and taking it in excess quantities will not necessarily increase its benefits.

Substitutes: There are other herbs that have adaptogenic benefits (like holy basil, for example), but they are not as well suited for smoothie uses. From a pure flavor standpoint, maca is difficult to replace. Though not true matches, possible substitutions include mesquite or carob powder. In truth, there really is no substitution for maca—it is in a class of "super" all its own.

Maqui Berries

Often called the "rainforest blueberry," maqui is a small purple berry that grows prolifically in certain areas of South America. Its color is incredibly vibrant and intense and can turn light-colored smoothies into stunning, violet creations that seem to glow. Taste-wise, maqui is very mild, especially when used in a dried form—in fact, some people report not being able to taste it at all. From a smoothie standpoint, this makes maqui a very versatile ingredient that can go into absolutely any blend at all as a superfood boost.

Buying: Maqui oxidizes quite quickly, so great care must be taken in commercial processing to preserve its nutrients. Because of this, freeze-dried maqui berry powder is your best bet in terms of offering optimum nutrition. The berries are picked, quickly juiced and milled, and then freeze-dried (a drying process that, like its name suggests, used very cold temperatures to extract the moisture without damaging nutrients). With this method, the nutrients in the maqui berry are suspended until it comes back in contact with water . . . or goes in a smoothie!

Benefits: Maqui berries' claim to fame is that, to date, they have the highest levels of antioxidants of any fruit ever tested—even higher than acai in terms of their rich anthocyanin content. This makes maqui an exceptional tool in any anti-aging arsenal, helping to neutralize free radicals and promote healthy circulation. They also contain many vitamins, especially vitamin C, and are naturally very low in sugar.

Serving Size: 2 teaspoons maqui powder.

Substitutes: Maqui has such a mild flavor that any substitution would be more about trying to replace some of its incredible benefits than taste. Acai berry, although not as high in antioxidants, is wonderful nonetheless and can be used just like maqui (I often think of acai and maqui as sister berries, even though botanically they are not). Blueberries can also be used as a kind of "poor man's" maqui (nutritionally speaking), containing, ounce for ounce, about a tenth of the antioxidants of maqui.

Mulberries

I'm from California, so imagine my surprise (and my jealousy) when I visited the East Coast for some superfood talks and encountered people saying, "We have mulberries growing in our backyard!" more times than I can count. Needless to say, if you have mulberries growing in your backyard, rejoice and use them in your smoothies! Or put them in your food dehydrator (or find a friend who has one and share the bounty), gently dry out your harvest, and have extra sweet mulberries on hand all year. Lucky you!

For the non-berry bestowed, mulberries look like small, elongated blackberries and are either dark purple or white. They have a watery, mildly sweet berry flavor when fresh, which is enhanced tremendously when dried. While most people put fresh mulberries in an ambivalent, "take it or leave it" flavor category, dried mulberries have a hard-core audience of obsessed fans (yours truly included). Incredible benefits aside, mulberries are one of my favorite secret ingredients in smoothies—they add a sweetness that compliments other flavors, from citrus to berry to vanilla, extremely well. Do note that if a smoothie containing a liberal quantity of dried mulberries (or any dried fruit for that matter) is allowed to sit for some period of time, it will thicken substantially, since the fruit swells as it slowly rehydrates. As a result, mulberries are best used in smoothies that will be consumed within the hour.

STORING SUPERFOOD INGREDIENTS

Since you're investing in top-quality ingredients, don't let them go to waste! Here's how to keep your top-tier superfoods at their peak:

Dried fruits (such as goji berries and mulberries): Store in glass containers such as mason jars (fruit may absorb plastic flavors with prolonged storage) and keep in a dark, dry place.

Fresh greens and sprouts (such as spinach and sunflower sprouts): Always keep fresh green produce in the crisper drawer of the refrigerator. Remove as much moisture as possible before storing; never wash greens ahead of time, unless you run them through a salad spinner to dry the leaves thoroughly.

Seeds, Nuts, and Acai Powder (ingredients containing healthy fats): Store in a sealable container (I use mason jars for these, too), and keep in the refrigerator or freezer for maximum shelf life.

Superfood powders (such as cacao, maca, and greens powders): Keep in a sealed, dry container (glass is best). Most powders may be stored at room temperature, preferably away from direct sunlight, and should always be kept away from moisture.

The best practice for storing superfood smoothie ingredients? When in doubt, seal it and freeze it. Many superfoods will remain usable far past their "best by" date when kept this way.

Buying: Fresh mulberries are available for a short period of time in some parts of the country, but their flavor is not the best for smoothies. Sun-dried mulberries, on the other hand, are an absolute dream when blended with other natural foods. Look for organic white Turkish mulberries—they're the sweetest.

Benefits: Mulberries are one of the best natural sources of resveratrol, a powerful and rare antioxidant that has been shown to help prevent aging, enhance cardiovascular health, and promote circulation. Also an excellent source of fiber, mulberries are a sweet treat with real benefits—they even contain protein!

Serving Size: 3 tablespoons sun-dried mulberries (about 1 ounce).

Substitutes: Although they offer no match for mulberries' resveratrol stores, raisins or dates can be used in place of mulberries at a 1:1 ratio.

North American Berries

Love berries? Fabulous—you are a lover of superfoods! While berries have been casually gathered since the days of our earliest ancestors, most berries have been actively cultivated for only a few hundred years. Now, there are thousands of local berry strains and species, with hundreds of types of blackberries alone. Berries are among the most nutrient-dense, locally available superfoods we have, and smoothies make regularly including them in your diet easier than ever. You can almost always add a handful of berries into a smoothie without disrupting (and actually often enhancing) the flavor. Perhaps the easiest superfood to incorporate, North American berries make a great first step in living a superfood lifestyle.

Varieties: North American berries are among the few truly indigenous superfood items of this continent. The recipes in this book rely on common varieties: strawberries, blueberries, blackberries, cranberries, and raspberries. That said, heirloom and regional selections are a welcome addition to smoothies! During the summertime, check your local farmers' market or a nearby road stand (or pick-your-own field, if you're lucky) for stunning gems such as white or black raspberries, lingonberries, or gooseberries.

Buying: I love fresh berries just as much as the next person, but I rarely use them in smoothies for three reasons: 1) They are expensive (the cost per smoothie ends up being a lot, since you'll generally need a cup or two of fresh berries); 2) They perish quickly; and 3) I am usually that person who eats all of them directly from the basket before I can even walk across the kitchen to the blender. Frozen berries, on the other hand, are a much better bargain at about half the cost, are often "fresher" than the ones on the store shelves since they are frozen very soon after harvest, and will last much longer stored in the freezer. For these reasons, the recipes in this book exclusively use frozen berries, which I strongly suggest stocking up on—it's a good reminder to make a smoothie every time you open that freezer door! Always make sure you buy organic berries as, unfortunately, berries are among the crops most heavily sprayed with pesticides (apparently we're not the only creatures that love berries). Although not used in the recipes in this book, freeze-dried berries can be an extra special addition to smoothies, as they retain most of their nutrition and add an especially concentrated berry flavor. They can be a fun smoothie-boosting experiment, although they are more expensive than regular frozen berries.

Benefits: The nutritional benefits of berries are the greatest when uncooked, making smoothies a perfect vehicle for consuming them. Berries act as little storage units of vitamins, particularly vitamins C and A, and contain some of the highest antioxidant levels of any fruits in the kingdom. They support the immune system, have anti-aging, anti-inflammatory properties, and provide excellent protection from disease.

Serving Size: 1 cup berries.

Substitutes: Although recipes are generally designed with the unique flavor of a specific berry in mind, it is usually easy to substitute one type of North American berry for another, so feel free to swap as needed.

Pomegranate

Truly an ancient fruit, embroidered into mythological tales, the pomegranate never ceases to amaze. With an exterior like a heavy red globe, the pomegranate's interior is packed with juicy, ruby-red kernels that have a delicate sweet-tart flavor. The edible seed on the inside of each "gem" offers a slightly nutty taste. If you have a very strong blender, using whole pomegranate seeds can be a special addition to smoothies, albeit a little crunchy. Without the aid of heavyweight blades and a powerful motor, however, pomegranate seeds will not blend at all, leaving large, chewy seeds throughout the smoothie. For this reason, the recipes in this book use pomegranate juice only—it's a bit easier to find, simpler to access (ever opened a pomegranate? Hint: Don't wear white), and more blender-friendly. Pomegranate has a beautiful tangy flavor when used in fruit blends, especially ones that feature berries or citrus.

Buying: Ideally, you'll find fresh pomegranate juice that has no added sugar and has not been watered down with other fruit juices stocked in the refrigerated section of your market. If this is unavailable, the next best option is a shelf-stable juice, again without any added sugars or juices—just pomegranate.

Benefits: One of the most heavily researched superfoods, pomegranate is a superstar of nutritional benefits. According to studies, drinking a glass of pomegranate juice a day can help protect against heart disease, cancer, and osteoarthritis.

With three times the amount of antioxidants found in red wine or green tea, along with powerful antiviral and antibacterial properties, pomegranate has been shown to be effective in fighting skin, lung, prostate, and breast cancer. It also has been proven to lower blood pressure and support cardiovascular health. And, hey, it's even high in healing vitamins like C, B1, and B2!

Serving Size: 6 to 8 ounces pomegranate juice.

Substitutes: Tart cherry juice makes a good substitute, and can be used at a 1:1 ratio. As a last resort, other juices such as grape or apple can be used in place of pomegranate, but are sweeter and do not offer any of the same benefits.

Sea Buckthorn Berries

Sea buckthorn sounds like some strange seaweed, but it's actually a pretty orange berry that grows in clusters along coastlines around the world, especially in Europe and Asia. Its short growing season, coupled with its thorny, sticky, and thus delicate harvesting process, all contribute to its high price point. Nonetheless, its benefits are so unique that it's worth finding ways to incorporate it—even if just on occasion.

The flavor of sea buckthorn is incomparable—citrusy, tart, and slightly oily (in a pleasant way), with mild floral flavor notes all rolled into a concentrated orange liquid. Sea buckthorn's complex flavor tends to stay prominently in the foreground of whatever smoothie it's in. Needless to say, it doesn't go with every flavor in the world, but it's receptive and intriguing when blended with sweet ingredients like citrus, tropical fruits, and even carrot juice.

Buying: Sea buckthorn berries are difficult to harvest and transport, and it is a rarity to encounter them fresh, at least in North America. The most convenient and readily available form for superfood smoothies is sea buckthorn juice—just be sure it's 100% pure juice, and not pre-sweetened. (See the Resource Guide on page 187 for the brand that I use.)

Benefits: Sea buckthorn is unique in its benefits, and is best known as a skin-regenerating food, even used for serious conditions like psoriasis. Very high in vitamin C, the anti-inflammatory antioxidant quercitin, and containing the exceptionally rare omega-7, sea buckthorn is a first-rate "beauty food."

Serving Size: 1 fluid ounce pure sea buckthorn juice.

Substitutes: From a simple flavor standpoint, orange juice with a squeeze of lemon juice makes a fair substitute, though this leaves most of sea buckthorn's benefits at the door. To be honest, there is not really an easy substitute for sea buckthorn juice. If you cannot obtain it, I'm inclined to suggest skipping the handful of recipes in this book that include it.

ADVENTUROUS SUPERFOODS

Because smoothies taste so good, blending your favorite (or soon-to-be favorite) superfood into the mix is a smart use of a mealtime. But there are many, many, more superfoods in the world outside of the "Super 15" just waiting to meet your blender (with new ones constantly being discovered). The list that follows is meant to be inspirational—most of these ingredients are not used in the smoothie recipes in this book, and many border on being considered medicinal herbs. Nonetheless, superfoods are a fascinating culinary adventure to explore, especially in the context of making superfood smoothies. It goes without saying: The healthy rewards of incorporating nature's finest foods are infinite.

Acerola cherry
Aloe
Baobab
Borojó
Caja
Cinnamon
Coffee berry
Cupuaçu
Elderberry
Ginger
Goldenberry (dried or powder)
Kelp
Lingonberry
Mangosteen
Matcha (powdered green tea)
Medicinal mushrooms (such as
    maitake, reishi, chaga, etc.)
Noni
Phytoplankton
Purple corn

Rice bran and germ
Sacha inchi
Sorghum bran
Tart cherry
Tocotrienol powder
Turmeric
Wheat germ
Yacon root

COST-CUTTING TECHNIQUES

It's entirely understandable to have moments of doubt when it comes to the cost of superfood ingredients. You may wonder, why spend $20 on a small bag of mysterious purple maqui berry powder when you could buy a burrito for six bucks? It can be a little daunting to place faith in these substantially more expensive items when you're initially building your collection of superfoods.

Despite their initial cost, however, superfoods are not actually as expensive as they seem. What you're really purchasing is nutrients—not calories and not quantity—and the cost per nutrient is actually substantially lower than many conventional "bargain" foods. These everyday staples are not necessarily bad (rice, for example, is a wonderful food!), but most simply cannot provide the wealth of nutrition that is needed to create your optimum state of health. If you want to be truly rich, invest in promoting a healthy body.

Nutrients aside, though, a superfood smoothie may seem like a pricey little drink, so here's an example of how it actually breaks down, looking at one of the premium recipes that uses the highest quantities of superfoods and thus is more expensive than most:

VANILLA ALMOND SMOOTHIE (PAGE 175)*

Dried white mulberries:	$1.14
Dried goji berries:	$.44
Hemp protein powder:	$.44
Lucuma powder:	$.83
Almond butter:	$.32
Vanilla extract:	$.41
Camu powder:	$.27
Coconut water:	$.88
Ice:	$0
Total cost per serving:	$4.73

* Costs reflect single-serving size, and are approximations based on full retail price. Better deals definitely exist, especially when buying online; your final cost will vary slightly.

As you can see, $4.73 is the actual cost of this superfood-dense smoothie, which is an easy meal replacement. And the unused ingredients will last a long time, allowing you to realize full value from your investment. It may not be as inexpensive as, say, a piece of toast, but there is simply no comparison in terms of the long-term benefits.

SOAKING INGREDIENTS FOR EASIER BLENDING

One of the benefits of a high-powered blender is that you can throw almost any ingredient inside and the machine will process it into a delightfully smooth concoction. Unfortunately, inexpensive or midrange blenders can sometimes struggle with breaking down denser ingredients, especially nuts, seeds, and dried fruit. Yet all is not lost if you're not using a high-powered blender. Soaking these types of ingredients prior to blending softens them, allowing the blender to work more effectively and alleviating chunky smoothie results. A bonus: Soaking nuts and seeds makes them even more digestible!

> **For nuts:** Place the nuts in a container and fill with twice as much water by volume. Soak for at least 2 hours and up to 1 day. Drain the water and rinse thoroughly. Soaked nuts will keep for several days in the refrigerator.
>
> **For large seeds** (such as sunflower seeds, pumpkin seeds): Place the seeds in a container and fill with twice as much water by volume. Soak for at least 1 hour and up to 1 day. Drain the water and rinse thoroughly. Soaked seeds will keep for several days in the refrigerator. (Note that soaked seeds will begin to sprout the longer they are left out—a great thing nutritionally speaking, although they contribute a "greener" flavor in smoothies.)
>
> **For small dried fruits:** Combine the fruits with the measured liquid used in the smoothie recipe (juice, coconut water, etc.). Soak for at least 15 minutes and up to 1 hour, until the fruit begins to plump up. Use the softened fruit and the soaking liquid in the smoothie for full flavor.
>
> **For dates:** Pit the dates, then mix them in with the measured liquid used in the smoothie recipe. Soak for at least 20 minutes and up to 1 day. Use the softened dates and the soaking liquid in the smoothie for full flavor.

For anyone looking to cut costs on making superfood smoothies, I have some good news for you: There are bona fide tricks of the trade. But getting the most bang for your buck requires committing to making a daily superfood smoothie part of your lifestyle, not just a one-time occurrence.

Buy frozen: Buying frozen fruits and vegetables is a drastically less expensive way to purchase produce for smoothies, sometimes with savings of more than 50%. Buying frozen also means that you'll reduce the risk of having your fresh produce spoil before you have the opportunity to use it.

Buy in bulk: Not every superfood is available, or practical, to buy in bulk, but many are. Seeds like hemp, chia, and flax are becoming more common in bulk bins in natural food stores. Many health websites offer larger sizes of their best-selling superfoods, like goji berries, which can be ordered at a significantly reduced rate per ounce. It's a bit of an investment up front, but you'll save a fortune in your daily regime. Keep a portion of the bulk superfoods out with your regular ingredients (I like to store them in glass jars—they're nice to look at), and seal up the rest to store in the freezer or refrigerator to maximize their shelf life.

Share: Find a smoothie buddy! You'll be surprised at how many friends, family members, roommates, or neighbors are not just willing, but *excited* to start a superfood smoothie journey with you. Find good deals on bulk orders of superfoods online (see the Resource Guide on page 187 for suggestions), and split the bill to get premium items at a fraction of the cost.

Let nothing go to waste: The worst thing you can possibly do is buy an expensive superfood item and let it collect dust. *That's* expensive. If you have surplus of a health food item or a superfood that you don't love the flavor of, add it in small, undetectable amounts to your daily smoothie. Just use it.

Make it at home: Since you're holding a book on how to make superfood smoothies, it's likely that making your own blends is already your intention. Nevertheless, it's important to realize and appreciate the real value of the smoothies that you're making. A typical smoothie bought at a shop or restaurant will usually cost around $5 or $6 for a 16-ounce serving. A superfood smoothie can cost $8 or $9; I've seen them for as much as $17 because of the ingredients used. Ordering a superfood smoothie while out is not a bad decision; I certainly do from time to time. But remember that you can easily make one at home that's a fraction of the cost and even, dare I say, more delicious. The recipes in this book will show you how.

TOOLS

It should come as no surprise to hear that in order to make smoothies, a blender is your indispensible kitchen tool. There was a time when blender options were fairly simple, but in recent years the popularity of smoothies (and the magic of blended items in other culinary capacities) has produced numerous choices in the art of blending. You can buy personal-size blenders, travel blenders, multitasking blenders (whose bases can be used for other tools like food processors), inexpensive drug-store blenders that cost less than a tank of gas, mid-price models, or high-powered blenders that cost more than a typical bicycle. I will readily admit my enthusiasm for such high-powered blenders—not out of lust for kitchen bling, but rather because these blenders are the workhorses of the blending world (they're

actually measured in horsepower!). They blend even the most temperamental produce items almost instantly and crush ice into the finest, frostiest bits for the most ideal smoothie texture imaginable. At the end of the day, they make whipping up smoothies easier, faster, and more fun. You may even find yourself more motivated to give produce a whirl when you've got a true blending mega-machine sitting on your counter. Personally, I use a Vitamix, though I think any brand at this top level is more than great. I have to say—I really, really love my blender, and think it's worth every penny (I do use it a lot!).

That said, you don't *need* a high-powered blender to make the recipes in this book. It's a great investment if you can swing it, but truth be told, a regular blender will do just fine. Cuisinart makes some excellent mid-level blenders that are aesthetically nice and get the job done. The most important thing is to get set up to make smoothies in the first place.

Other than a blender (and of course our superfood ingredients!), there are not many things you will need to make the recipes in this book. A few ice cube trays are useful to make some of the flavored ices; get the ones with covers if possible so you can keep the ice from absorbing other flavors in the freezer (see page 187 for source recommendations). A citrus zester is a helpful and inexpensive tool, but you can use a regular vegetable grater (using the finest grate) as well. A sharp knife (and decent cutting board) is always essential. And that's really all there is to it.

THE NUTRITIONAL REWARDS OF SMOOTHIES

Though the recipes in this book are categorized by flavor profile, the health benefits are just as important. For this reason, you'll notice a series of icons beneath each smoothie recipe, denoting the particular health benefits of that recipe: protein, low-calorie, immunity, beauty, cleanse/detox, heart health, and bone strength. Believe me, there are *far* more benefits to these recipes than what these icons represent. To keep things simple, in this section you'll find a run-down on a few of the exciting things you can expect from your superfood smoothies.

BUILT-IN BENEFITS

One of the many luxuries of drinking superfood smoothies is knowing that there are certain benefits you will always be accruing by incorporating more whole, raw, nutrient-dense, plant-based foods into your diet. Since these merits are an attribute of every smoothie in the book, there are no icons to reflect that the smoothie provides them. Rather, they are the ongoing result of consuming all of these incredible foods and ingredients. Here are some of the health perks you'll gain from every recipe:

Energy: While we can't make more time in the day, we can help our bodies have more energy to achieve our daily goals and responsibilities. Consuming a superfood smoothie every day is a little like having a delicious form of insurance that at least one of the day's meals will be saturated with exceptional nutrition. Many people report feeling lighter, stronger, more focused, and, of course, more energized after drinking a superfood smoothie— an outcome that influences the rest of the day. It's a key reason why many people turn to superfood smoothies in the first place, and why they return again and again. Once you experience the lasting energy drinking a superfood smoothie gives you, you'll understand what all the fuss is about!

Anti-aging Antioxidants: Whole, plant-based foods and superfoods contain nutrients that support cellular health on an overall level, helping maintain and achieve optimum wellness. Many of these foods are impressively high in antioxidants, which aid in protecting the body against the ravages of time at any age, while also strengthening just about every system in the body. There isn't a smoothie in this book that doesn't contain antioxidants, helping to fight cell-damaging free radicals and protecting against future damage. Antioxidants keep free radicals from forming in the first place, wipe out current oxidants, help remove damaged molecules, clean up toxins, and prevent future oxidation (that is, when the body begins to "rust").

The ORAC (Oxygen Radical Absorbance Capacity) scale is used to quantify antioxidant levels in foods. Though there are many nuances in nutrition that join forces to provide therapeutic benefits, high ORAC values are a wonderful indication of a beneficial food. Here's a breakdown of how many of our favorite superfoods stack up to help us turn back the clock.

INGREDIENT	ORAC*
Cacao powder (100 grams)	95,000
Maqui berry powder (100 grams)	60,600
Acai berry powder (100 grams)	53,600
Sun-dried goji berries (100 grams)	13,300
Blueberries (½ cup)	6,552
Strawberries (½ cup)	3,577
Spinach (1 cup raw)	3,030
Pomegranate (½ cup juice)	2,341
Kale (1 cup raw)	1,770
Carrots (½ cup)	666
Tomatoes (½ cup)	367
Mangos (½ cup)	300

*ORAC value is an estimate subject to variance depending on source, growing region, processing procedure, and freshness.

Vitamins and Minerals: Superfoods overflow with vitamins and minerals, often the same ones that are so often lacking in our modern diet. Delivering the micronutrients our bodies need is an inherent part of the superfood smoothie package and, once again, every one of these smoothies contains them. Enjoy a diversity of recipes with varied sets of ingredients for the quickest path to overall health. For an idea of how some of the top superfoods stack up in terms of the most sought-after micronutrients, refer back to the individual benefit sections of the "Super 15" superfoods on pages 16–33.

BONUS BENEFITS

In addition to the built-in benefits of drinking superfood smoothies, most of the recipes are particularly valuable in addressing specific health conditions. You can use the icons found on every recipe to view the power of a smoothie at a glance. Below you will find a guide to the rewards associated with each icon. And check out the handy Smoothies by Benefit Index starting on page 190 if you need to find a smoothie to serve a specific function.

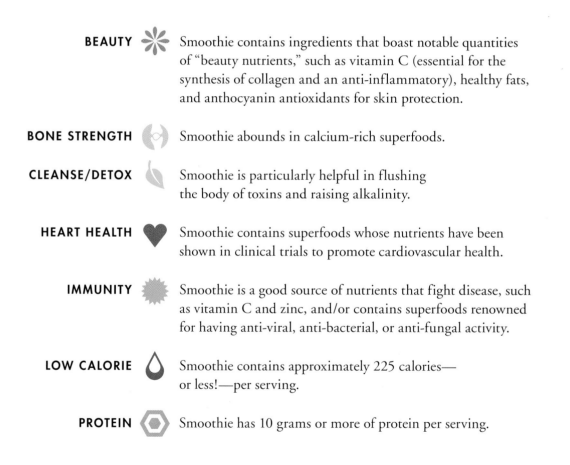

BEAUTY Smoothie contains ingredients that boast notable quantities of "beauty nutrients," such as vitamin C (essential for the synthesis of collagen and an anti-inflammatory), healthy fats, and anthocyanin antioxidants for skin protection.

BONE STRENGTH Smoothie abounds in calcium-rich superfoods.

CLEANSE/DETOX Smoothie is particularly helpful in flushing the body of toxins and raising alkalinity.

HEART HEALTH Smoothie contains superfoods whose nutrients have been shown in clinical trials to promote cardiovascular health.

IMMUNITY Smoothie is a good source of nutrients that fight disease, such as vitamin C and zinc, and/or contains superfoods renowned for having anti-viral, anti-bacterial, or anti-fungal activity.

LOW CALORIE Smoothie contains approximately 225 calories— or less!—per serving.

PROTEIN Smoothie has 10 grams or more of protein per serving.

USING SUPERFOOD SMOOTHIES
TO ACHIEVE A HEALTHY WEIGHT

As any person in the food industry will tell you, working with edible items all day may be wonderful (for foodies like me, it's a dream!), but it has one potentially big downside: You end up eating *a lot*! Constant taste-tests add up unconsciously and quickly, which can compromise energy and easily sneak on unwanted pounds. Yet, a funny thing happened to me while writing this book.

It may all sound terribly cliché, but after weeks and weeks of making smoothies all day every day, I began to experience a noticeable increase in energy. I was more productive, and I was able to think more clearly, pursue athletic activities with more vigor, and pack extra fun into each day. I felt capable of just a little bit *more*. But the real cherry on top (of the smoothie, of course) was what I discovered right after I finished putting together the book. Although my food consumption increased temporarily while recipe testing, not only did my weight stay the same, but I was in fact leaner: A test at the gym revealed that my body fat percentage had dropped a few notches. I was amazed. It was as if my body had been gently tweaked into an improved state of balance—an incredibly motivating result achieved by an effortless, delicious activity!

Incorporating superfood smoothies into your diet as a means to help reach weight loss goals is a smart move. Many of them can be treated as a full meal, shaving calories off your daily budget and gaining an immense amount of nutrition. Because superfood smoothies are so nutritionally dense, they keep us feeling satisfied longer, as the body has everything it needs to perform well. Plus, unlike many diets or cleanses, superfood smoothies provide the energy we need to thrive during the day. It's a virtuous cycle: More energy leads to more activity, which leads to looking and feeling better, which leads to craving healthier foods like superfood smoothies . . . and the process continues down its positive road. Whether you use superfood smoothies exclusively as a daily way to upgrade your health or you incorporate them as part of a more intensive diet or cleanse plan, they undoubtedly have the potential to help transform you into your optimum self.

PART TWO

THE SMOOTHIES

The expansive variety of natural foods available to us these days translates to a seemingly limitless range of superfood smoothies, both in form and function. In the following pages you'll find fruit-packed and refreshing drinks in the Fruity & Light section; create cleansing and invigorating blends from the Green & Vibrant recipes; enjoy luscious Rich & Creamy shakes; encounter epic superfood extravaganzas with the Premium Blends; and learn extra-functional superfood alchemy using the Superfood Shots recipes. What's your smoothie style? A world of energizing possibilities awaits you.

HOW MUCH SMOOTHIE SHOULD I DRINK?

Activity level, body size, metabolism rate, and many other factors come into play when determining serving sizes. For the average person, the recipes in this book make about two servings. You'll notice some servings are larger than others—12 ounces versus 16 ounces, for example—primarily due to the lightness or richness (and thus calorie content) of the ingredients used. Most people find that a serving or two of a superfood smoothie every day is the best for energy, and consuming a variety of smoothies over the course of the week is best for long-term balance.

Despite this serving recommendation, I encourage you to use the best calculator of all: your own instincts. Every one of these blends includes some of the most optimum foods you can possibly put into your body; they do not require the same level of careful regimen as say, a chocolate cake might. Because they are made with whole foods, they do not contain isolated supplements or artificial ingredients that can cause biological stress in high doses. I think that's one of the true beauties of superfood smoothies: We can leave our calculated measurements at the door, relax, and simply enjoy until satisfied.

TIPS TO REMEMBER

- Just as no two snowflakes are identical, no two apples are exactly alike. Produce can vary dramatically in flavor, sweetness, size, and even color. One banana may be sweeter than another, or one bundle of kale might have more of a "bite" than one picked later in the season. Always taste your smoothie before pouring it to make sure it's what you want in terms of flavor, and don't be afraid to make adjustments. Often the best smoothies are the ever-so-slightly tweaked ones.

- If you'd like more flavor out of a blend, or just want it to be sweeter, adjust it by prudently adding one of the sweeteners mentioned on page 10–12. Recipes that list a sweetener as optional are naturally quite sweet, but, as master of your own blender, I encourage you to be the judge.

- If a smoothie tastes too sweet for your liking, add additional water, ice, greens, or healthy fats (such as nuts) to bring it back into balance.

- Always use nuts and seeds with their hulls fully removed and with no added salt. Nut butters like almond butter should also be unsalted and unsweetened.

- When buying nondairy milks, always choose unsweetened, unflavored varieties, or look for the lowest sugar option available.

- The coconut milk called for in these recipes is the boxed variety, not the much richer canned version. If unavailable, mix ¼ cup canned coconut milk with ¾ cup water as a substitute for 1 cup boxed coconut milk.

- Citrus zest refers to grated citrus peel. Use a zester or the finest slots on a grater, grating only the colored portion of the peel and not the bitter white pith.

- If, while making smoothies, you have trouble blending, try the soaking technique described on page 35 to help soften the ingredients. You can always leave them to soak directly in the blender if the smoothie is already partially made.

- Make smoothies frostier by adding more ice or frozen produce. Make them thinner by adding water, juice, or a nondairy milk.

- All the superfood smoothie recipes in this book make approximately 2 servings. If you're looking to make a smoothie for just one person, simply cut the recipe in half.

FRUITY & LIGHT

Refreshing, hydrating, and bursting with sun-kissed fruit, Fruity and Light superfood smoothies take advantage of nature's sweetest bounty. Featured superfoods include mild-flavored maqui and camu berry powders, dried superberries like goji and mulberries, frozen North American berries, and often chia and flaxseed to add extra fiber and slow down the release of fruit sugars for more sustainable energy. These smoothie blends are especially enjoyable as a light breakfast or an energizing midday snack.

= FEATURED SUPERFOOD INGREDIENT

BEAUTY   BONE STRENGTH   CLEANSE/DETOX

HEART HEALTH   IMMUNITY   LOW CALORIE   PROTEIN

HONEYDEW MAQUI

Like anything melon-oriented, the more in-season and ripe your honeydew, the more glorious the resulting smoothie will be. This blend absolutely begs for a nice summer day, preferably sans shoes.

MAKES 2 16-OUNCE SERVINGS

3 cups honeydew melon, cubed

½ cup coconut milk (boxed variety)

2 teaspoons maqui berry powder

1 tablespoon flaxseed powder

1 tablespoon freshly squeezed lime juice

2 cups coconut ice (page 11)

sweetener, to taste

Blend all the ingredients together until smooth. Taste, and adjust sweetness if desired.

SUPERFOOD BOOST
Add 1 teaspoon of wheatgrass powder to sneak in extra greens.

STRAWBERRY CHAMOMILE

Sometimes when I make tea at night, I'll make an extra cup or two and toss it in the refrigerator, saving it for a morning smoothie. The slightly sweet and floral flavor of chamomile is a gorgeous match for bright, juicy strawberries.

MAKES 2 16-OUNCE SERVINGS

- 2 cups frozen strawberries
- ½ cup dried white mulberries
- 1¾ cups brewed chamomile tea (chilled)
- 2 tablespoons freshly squeezed lemon juice
- sweetener, to taste (optional)
- 2 tablespoons chia seeds

Blend the strawberries, mulberries, tea, and lemon juice together until smooth. Stop the blender, taste, and add desired sweetener if needed. Add the chia seeds, and give the blender a second quick whirl, just to mix the ingredients. (Incorporating the chia seeds at the end allows the smoothie to retain a smoother texture.)

SUPERFOOD BOOST
Add ½ teaspoon of camu berry powder for a vitamin C boost.

ACAI PUMPKIN

Though creamy, this energizing smoothie is surprisingly light and would make a successful breakfast or pre-workout smoothie, thanks to its electrolytes, antioxidants, and sustainable complex carbohydrates.

MAKES 2 10-OUNCE SERVINGS

½ cup canned pumpkin puree, unsweetened

¼ cup Medjool dates, pitted (about 3–4 large fruits)

3 tablespoons acai powder

1 cup coconut water

1 cup ice

sweetener, to taste (optional)

Blend all the ingredients together, except for the ice, until smooth. Add the ice and blend until frosty. Taste, and adjust sweetness if desired.

SUPERFOOD BOOST
Add 2 tablespoons of ground flaxseed for additional fiber and healthy fats.

ORANGE GOJI

You can practically spot the vibrancy of this superfruit smoothie a mile away. In addition to tasting like tangy, fruity paradise, it also contains many immune-boosting foods, including oranges, goji berries, and limes.

MAKES 2 16-OUNCE SERVINGS

2 peeled, de-seeded, and chopped oranges

1 frozen banana (see below)

⅓ cup dried goji berries

2 tablespoons hemp seeds

½ cup coconut water

¼ cup freshly squeezed lime juice

2 cups ice

sweetener, to taste (optional)

Blend all the ingredients together, except for the ice, until smooth. Add the ice and blend once more until frosty. Taste, and adjust sweetness if desired.

SUPERFOOD BOOST
Add 2 tablespoons of chia seeds to slow down the release of fruit sugars into the bloodstream, promoting sustainable energy.

FROZEN BANANAS

Using frozen bananas creates rich, frosty, healthy smoothies. Make a big batch so you'll have this special ingredient on hand for weeks to come. For best results, follow these tips:

- Use the brownest, ripest bananas you can find—they become truly delicious when frozen.
- Before freezing, remove the banana peel, cut the fruit into pieces, and lay flat inside

a sealable plastic freezer bag. This retains freshness and makes the banana pieces easier to work with.

- When cutting the bananas, be consistent—this simplifies measuring later. For example, you might decide to always cut bananas into sixths, so when a recipe calls for "one frozen banana," you know how many pieces to include to create an entire banana.

WATERMELON ACAI

Watermelon smoothies are one of my favorite drinkable treats, and this superfood-infused version provides a whole new symphony of flavor—and antioxidant-rich nutrition. For an extra-frosty smoothie, freeze the watermelon cubes before blending (a good way to help preserve the aftermath of overzealous melon purchases, too).

MAKES 2 20-OUNCE SERVINGS

5 cups cubed seedless watermelon

2 tablespoons acai powder

3 tablespoons chia seeds

1 teaspoon freshly grated lemon zest

2 tablespoons freshly squeezed lemon juice

¼ cup pure pomegranate juice

2½ cups ice

sweetener, to taste

Blend all the ingredients together until smooth. Taste, and adjust sweetness if desired.

....

SUPERFOOD BOOST
Add ½ teaspoon camu powder for an additional boost of almost 600% RDA vitamin C.

....

MAQUI BERRY PEACH

*There isn't a peach recipe in the world that can compete with the divinity
of a freshly picked, perfectly ripe, drip-down-your-arm-juicy peach. Nonetheless,
peaches add a lovely creamy touch to smoothies, and the subtle hint of berry
from the maqui berry powder makes for a fun and flirty flavor match.*

MAKES 2 12-OUNCE SERVINGS

1½ cups frozen peaches

2 teaspoons maqui berry powder

½ teaspoon camu berry powder

1 tablespoon freshly squeezed
lemon juice

½ teaspoon vanilla extract

2 cups rice milk (original variety)

sweetener, to taste

Blend all the ingredients together until smooth. Taste, and adjust
sweetness as desired.

SUPERFOOD BOOST
Add 2 tablespoons dried goji berries.

SEA BUCKTHORN CARROT

In Russia, sea buckthorn berries are often used in a creamy drink concocted from fresh berries, carrot juice, and buttermilk—which may appear to be a questionable combination, but is surprisingly addicting. This recipe superfood-izes this intriguing beverage and turns it into a deeply refreshing smoothie . . . with exceptional (and, dare I say, improved) results.

MAKES 2 16-OUNCE SERVINGS

⅓ cup raw cashews

¼ cup Medjool dates, pitted (about 3–4 large fruits)

1½ cups fresh carrot juice

¼ cup sea buckthorn juice

2 cups coconut ice (page 11)

1 cup ice

sweetener, to taste (optional)

Blend the cashews, dates, carrot juice, and sea buckthorn juice together until creamy. Add the two types of ice and blend once more until frosty. Though it's already inherently sweet, taste, and adjust the sweetness of the smoothie according to your preference.

....

SUPERFOOD BOOST
Add 3 tablespoons chia seeds to add
extra fiber for long-term satiation.

....

PINEAPPLE PAPAYA

*Delicately sweet, papaya makes this smoothie creamy yet pleasantly light.
The softer and riper the papaya, the more worthy it is of this smoothie.*

MAKES 2 16-OUNCE SERVINGS

1 cup frozen pineapple chunks

1⅓ cups peeled, de-seeded, and chopped fresh papaya

⅓ cup dried goji berries

2 tablespoons lucuma powder

⅓ cup freshly squeezed lime juice

1¼ cups coconut milk (boxed variety)

sweetener, to taste

Blend all the ingredients together until smooth. Taste, and blend in sweetener as desired.

SUPERFOOD BOOST
Add 1 teaspoon wheatgrass powder for nourishing detoxification.

POMEGRANATE ORANGE

*The eye-opening natural flavors of this fruity blend
are quick to shake up a tired smoothie routine.*

MAKES 2 12-OUNCE SERVINGS

1 peeled, de-seeded, and
chopped orange

✳ 2 tablespoons dried goji berries

¾ teaspoon freshly grated
orange zest

¼ teaspoon cinnamon powder

✳ ¾ cup pomegranate juice

2 cups almond ice (page 11)

sweetener, to taste

Blend all the ingredients together until smooth and frosty. Taste, and blend in sweetener as desired.

SUPERFOOD BOOST

Add 2 tablespoons hemp seeds to balance out the nutrition
with some extra-healthy essential fatty acids.

STRAWBERRY KOMBUCHA

Simple and delicate, this blend reminds me of strawberries and champagne . . . but the kind you can enjoy at two in the afternoon on a Monday. Kombucha is a fermented drink that is wonderful for digestion; you can find it in the refrigerated section at most health stores.

MAKES 2 12-OUNCE SERVINGS

2 cups frozen strawberries

2 cups kombucha (original flavor)

2 teaspoons maqui berry powder

sweetener, to taste

1 tablespoon chia seeds

Blend the strawberries, kombucha, and maqui berry powder together. Taste, sweeten if desired, then add the chia seeds. Give the mixture a brief blend, just to mix it.

SUPERFOOD BOOST
Add 2 tablespoons dried goji berries.

BLUEBERRY GOJI

Green tea and chia gel help make this tranquil smoothie extra light and energizing.

MAKES 2 16-OUNCE SERVINGS

- 3 tablespoons dried goji berries
- ¼ cup Medjool dates, pitted (about 3–4 large fruits)
- 1½ cups prepared green tea (chilled)
- 1 cup frozen blueberries
- 1 cup frozen strawberries
- 1 teaspoon vanilla extract
- ½ cup chia gel (page 21)
- sweetener, to taste (optional)

Blend the goji berries, dates, and green tea together until smooth. Add the remaining ingredients and blend again until frosty. Taste, and sweeten as desired.

SUPERFOOD BOOST
Add 1 teaspoon maqui berry powder.

RASPBERRY PEACH

*A drink as summery as summer can be! Depending on the natural sugars in your fruit,
this blend can potentially benefit from an extra touch of sweetener to enhance the flavors.*

MAKES 2 16-OUNCE SERVINGS

1½ cups fresh peaches, pitted
and chopped

1½ cups frozen raspberries

¼ cup Medjool dates, pitted
(about 3–4 large fruits)

1 cup unsweetened almond milk

2 tablespoons chia seeds

¼ teaspoon vanilla extract

2 cups ice

sweetener, to taste

Blend together all the ingredients, except the ice, until smooth.
Add the ice and blend again until frosty. Taste, and sweeten as
desired.

SUPERFOOD BOOST
Use dried mulberries in place of the dates.

CRANBERRY ORANGE

Flavor lovers, *that's what cranberries and oranges are . . . and the inclusion of goji berries
makes for an ideal ménage à trois. But in smoothies there's always room for one more,
so I love adding the optional superfood boost of acai into this mix, as well.*

MAKES 2 16-OUNCE SERVINGS

- ¾ cup fresh or frozen whole cranberries
- ¼ cup dried goji berries
- 1 cup chopped ripe pear
- 1 tablespoon flaxseed powder
- 1½ cups orange juice
- 2 cups ice
- sweetener, to taste (optional)

Blend all the ingredients together, except the ice, until smooth. Add the ice and blend again until frosty. Taste, and sweeten as desired.

SUPERFOOD BOOST
Add 1 tablespoon acai powder.

COCONUT GOJI

If you've never steeped a couple of tablespoons of goji berries in coconut water before—drinking the sweet, complex, hydrating "tea," and relishing the plumped berries as an after-drink treat—I respectfully ask you to put down this book and go do it now. (Soak for 15–30 minutes before consuming.) The recipe below is the smoothie version of this simple pleasure . . . and it reminds me a little of the most delicious fresh-pressed carrot juice ever (likely because of the massive quantity of carotene antioxidants found in goji berries).

MAKES 2 12-OUNCE SERVINGS

⅓ cup dried goji berries

¼ cup shredded coconut
(unsweetened)

2 tablespoons hemp seeds

1 cup coconut water

2 cups coconut ice (page 11)

sweetener, to taste (optional)

Blend all the ingredients, except the ice, together until smooth. Add the ice and blend again until frosty. Taste, and sweeten as desired.

SUPERFOOD BOOST
Though it's not one of our featured superfoods, adding a bit of anti-inflammatory ginger is a wonderful addition to this smoothie. Use to taste.

RHUBARB MINT

Rhubarb is reserved most often for an appearance in the quintessential baked pie, but I love using it unheated, allowing it to offer a tangy element that's a fun, fresh flavor for smoothies. You can buy frozen rhubarb at many stores, or simply chop it up fresh and freeze it yourself. (Note that the leaves of rhubarb are poisonous, so make sure to only use the red stalk.)

MAKES 2 16-OUNCE SERVINGS

1½ cups frozen rhubarb

⅓ cup dried goji berries

¼ cup Medjool dates, pitted (about 3–4 large fruits)

¼ cup hemp seeds

1 tablespoon (packed) minced fresh mint

1½ cups orange juice

2 cups ice

sweetener, to taste

Blend together all the ingredients, except the ice, until smooth. Add the ice and blend again until frosty. Taste, and sweeten as desired.

···

SUPERFOOD BOOST
Add ½ teaspoon camu powder.

···

PEACHES & CREAM

Fresh peaches offer so much more flavor than frozen peaches—there's really no comparison, especially when they're in peak season. And during the summer months, when I've likely bought far too many peaches to eat in a reasonable amount of time, this smoothie becomes a regular on the daily menu. I like it best with a little extra stevia, which enhances the peach flavor even further.

MAKES 2 16-OUNCE SERVINGS

3 cups chopped fresh peaches, pitted

1 frozen banana (page 51)

❋ 1 tablespoon chia seeds

❋ 1 tablespoon goji berries

2 cups coconut milk

1 tablespoon freshly squeezed lemon juice

½ teaspoon vanilla extract

sweetener, to taste

Blend all the ingredients together until smooth. Taste, and sweeten as desired.

....

SUPERFOOD BOOST
Add 1 tablespoon hemp seeds.

....

MULBERRY PLUM

When you're stoning plums (or peaches, or any stone fruit for that matter), do it over the same bowl into which you're putting the fruit flesh. This way, you'll get every last drop of delicious fresh juice right where it belongs: in the smoothie.

MAKES 2 16-OUNCE SERVINGS

¾ cup frozen strawberries

¾ cup frozen cherries

¼ cup dried white mulberries

1½ cups cubed plums, pitted

2 tablespoons acai powder

½ cup water

1 teaspoon vanilla extract

1 cup ice

sweetener, to taste

Blend all the ingredients together, except the ice, until smooth. Add the ice and blend again until frosty. Taste, and sweeten as desired.

SUPERFOOD BOOST
Add 2 tablespoons hemp seeds.

SEA BUCKTHORN FIG

I briefly lived in a house with a fig tree out front, which caused three Augusts of my life to be an epic battle of the greediest: me against the squirrels. Sadly, the squirrels and I never came to a reasonable solution, but I did learn the joy of blending ultra-ripe figs into thick smoothies, which have a tendency to create a demurely sweet creaminess that's usually reserved for heavier ingredients. It's the perfect complement to sea buckthorn's slightly pucker-inducing taste, resulting in a complex-flavored smoothie with many notes.

MAKES 2 16-OUNCE SERVINGS

1½ cups fresh figs, de-stemmed and quartered

2 large Medjool dates, pitted

3 tablespoons sea buckthorn juice

1 tablespoon lucuma powder

½ tablespoon almond butter

½ cup apple juice

½ cup unsweetened almond milk

2 cups ice

sweetener, to taste

Blend together all the ingredients, except the ice, until smooth. Add the ice and blend again until frosty. Taste, and sweeten as desired.

SUPERFOOD BOOST
Add 2 tablespoons chia seeds.

CANTALOUPE PEACH

The soft flavors of juicy summer fruit join forces in this refreshing, rejuvenating blend.

MAKES 2 16-OUNCE SERVINGS

1 cup chopped cantaloupe

1 cup frozen strawberries

2 cups chopped peaches

2 tablespoons lucuma powder

¼ teaspoon camu powder

2 tablespoons sea buckthorn juice

1 cup coconut water

¼ cup freshly squeezed lime juice

sweetener, to taste

Blend the cantaloupe into a juice by itself first. Add the remaining ingredients and blend again until frosty. Taste, and sweeten as desired.

SUPERFOOD BOOST
Add 1 teaspoon wheatgrass powder or greens blend.

GRAPEFRUIT POMEGRANATE

Grapefruit has a domineering flavor that likes to be the center of attention—one of the reasons it is seldom used in smoothies, which is more of a team sport. Here, although it still takes the spotlight, grapefruit works nicely with the other fruits, resulting in a full-bodied flavor.

MAKES 2 14-OUNCE SERVINGS

- 2 cups frozen strawberries
- 1½ cups green tea ice (page 11)
- 1 cup grapefruit, peeled, de-seeded, and chopped
- 1½ cups pomegranate juice
- 2 teaspoons maqui berry powder
- ½ teaspoon ginger powder
- sweetener, to taste

Blend all the ingredients together until frosty. Taste, and sweeten as desired.

SUPERFOOD BOOST
Add 2 tablespoons hemp seeds.

STRAWBERRY CUCUMBER

Low in sugar, extra hydrating, and full of beauty-enriching minerals, the ingredients in this light and bright recipe are all glow-enhancing foods. Don't be shy about adding a little sweetener to bring the flavors to new heights.

MAKES 2 16-OUNCE SERVINGS

2 cups frozen strawberries

2 cups peeled and chopped cucumber

¼ cup chopped celery

¼ cup raw cashews

2 tablespoons freshly squeezed lemon juice

½ teaspoon (packed) minced fresh mint

1 cup water

sweetener, to taste

Blend all the ingredients together until smooth. Taste, and sweeten as desired.

SUPERFOOD BOOST
Add 2 tablespoons dried goji berries.

CARROT CARDAMOM

There's something so exciting about cardamom—it has a more uplifting, fresher feeling than many of the warmer spices like nutmeg or even cinnamon. Along with sunflower seeds (which create the most delicious "milk" when blended with water), it makes this sweet carrot smoothie quite special. I nudge you to try this smoothie with the optional boost of cacao nibs for an unexpectedly stunning combination of flavor.

MAKES 2 16-OUNCE SERVINGS

¼ cup sunflower seeds

1½ cups coconut water

1 frozen banana (page 51)

2 cups ice

2 tablespoons goji berries

1 tablespoon ground flaxseed powder

¼ teaspoon cardamom powder

½ cup carrot juice

sweetener, to taste

Blend the sunflower seeds and coconut water together into a smooth "milk." Add the remaining ingredients and blend until smooth. Taste, and sweeten as desired.

SUPERFOOD BOOST
After blending the smoothie as described above, add ¼ cup cacao nibs. Blend until nibs are broken down, but still maintain a little crunch.

MANGO CHILI

*Sweet and tropical with a hint of spice, the key to making this smoothie is using a
chili powder made exclusively from red chiles—not one that's a blend of other spices
(like oregano and garlic), which offer too much of a savory flavor for smoothie purposes.
If you can't find a pure chili powder, use a fresh, de-seeded, red jalapeño pepper instead.*

MAKES 2 16-OUNCE SERVINGS

2½ cups frozen mango chunks

3 tablespoons hemp seeds

2 tablespoons dried goji berries

1 teaspoon chili powder (see
note above)

1½ cups apple juice

1 cup water

2 tablespoons freshly squeezed
lime juice

sweetener, to taste (optional)

Blend all the ingredients together until smooth. Taste, and blend in
sweetener as desired.

SUPERFOOD BOOST
Add 1 tablespoon chia seeds for extra fiber.

GREEN & VIBRANT

Ranging from sweet to peppery, the green smoothie revolution is quickly on the rise, and for good reason. Boost a healthy smoothie with green leafy vegetables. Amazingly, leafy greens blend in so seamlessly with flavorful fruits and superfoods that the only reminder of their beneficial presence is the smoothie's trademark bright green color. Fresh and frozen leafy greens of all varieties make great additions, as do freeze-dried powders like wheatgrass, and even the occasional chlorella or spirulina boost. With benefits galore, these blends are revolutionary tools for those looking to add a little more green into their diet. Providing energy you can feel, green smoothies are a great way to begin the day, but can be enjoyed at any time . . . even as a light dinner.

� = FEATURED SUPERFOOD INGREDIENT

✳ BEAUTY   ◎ BONE STRENGTH   ◁ CLEANSE/DETOX

♥ HEART HEALTH   ✺ IMMUNITY   ◊ LOW CALORIE   ⬡ PROTEIN

BANANA ROMAINE

*Romaine's light flavor makes it a breeze to whirl into a smoothie—I especially like
using the romaine hearts for smoothies due to their mildness. Feel free to trade
the chlorella for another condensed greens powder, like wheatgrass.*

MAKES 2 16-OUNCE SERVINGS

2 frozen bananas (page 51)

3 cups (packed) romaine lettuce
leaves, finely chopped

½ teaspoon chlorella powder

1 teaspoon vanilla extract

1½ cups coconut water

1 cup almond ice (page 11)

sweetener, to taste

Blend all the ingredients together until smooth. Taste, and adjust
sweetness as desired.

SUPERFOOD BOOST
Add 1 tablespoon acai powder for anthocyanin antioxidants.

GINGER PEAR

*The green color of this smoothie may give the nutritional benefits away,
but the fruit and the fresh ginger are the only flavors that come through.
To maximize sweetness, allow your pears to ripen fully, until very soft.*

MAKES 2 12-OUNCE SERVINGS

2 cups diced ripe pear

⅓ cup dried white mulberries

2 teaspoons freshly minced
peeled ginger

2 cups chopped frozen spinach

1¾ cups unsweetened almond
milk

sweetener, to taste

Blend all the ingredients together until smooth. Taste, and adjust sweetness if desired.

SUPERFOOD BOOST
Add 2 tablespoons of hemp seeds for healthy fats and protein.

CUCUMBER MINT

The epitome of refreshing, this gorgeous blend is deeply cooling and a wonderful drink for the skin. I like to use just a touch of sweetener and let the delicate flavor of the cucumber speak for itself. If your cucumber is organic, you can use the skin in the smoothie for extra minerals.

MAKES 2 16-OUNCE SERVINGS

3 cups diced cucumber (peeled, if not organic)

¼ cup raw cashews

¼ cup (packed) chopped fresh mint leaves

2 cups packed baby spinach

1 tablespoon freshly squeezed lemon juice

3 cups coconut ice (page 11)

sweetener, to taste (optional)

Blend together all the ingredients, except the coconut ice, until smooth. Add the coconut ice and blend once more. Sweeten to taste.

SUPERFOOD BOOST
Add ½ teaspoon camu powder for an extra skin-healthy vitamin C boost.

APPLE ARUGULA

*Rather than try and hide the bold flavor of arugula, this light green
smoothie celebrates it in a refreshing, crisp-tasting blend.*

MAKES 2 16-OUNCE SERVINGS

1 very ripe pear

2 tablespoons hemp seeds

1 cup (packed) arugula leaves

3 tablespoons freshly squeezed
lemon juice

1½ cups apple juice

1 cup ice

sweetener, to taste

Blend all the ingredients together until smooth. Taste, and sweeten
as desired.

SUPERFOOD BOOST
Add ½ teaspoon camu powder.

MANGO COCONUT

Light green in hue and refreshing in taste, this smoothie is a great recipe for anyone who loves the idea of a green smoothie but wants to start slow since the wheatgrass is completely undetectable.

MAKES 2 16-OUNCE SERVINGS

1½ cups frozen mango chunks

1 cup coconut ice (page 11)

1½ cups coconut milk (boxed variety)

1 very ripe pear

1½ tablespoons lucuma powder

1 teaspoon wheatgrass powder

2 tablespoons chia seeds

sweetener, to taste

Blend all the ingredients together until smooth. Taste, and sweeten as desired.

SUPERFOOD BOOST

Add ½ teaspoon camu powder.

LUCUMA LIME

For such a creamy treat, you'd almost think there was yogurt in this blend!

MAKES 2 16-OUNCE SERVINGS

1½ cups frozen spinach

1 frozen banana (page 51)

3 tablespoons mashed avocado

2 tablespoons lucuma powder

¼ cup freshly squeezed lime juice

2 cups coconut water

sweetener, to taste

Blend all the ingredients together until smooth. Taste, and sweeten as desired.

SUPERFOOD BOOST
Add 2 tablespoons hemp protein powder.

SWEET ALMOND

*This delicate blend is almost like a milkshake—mostly due to using frozen spinach
as a nearly flavorless textural agent. If you have almond extract on hand (yum),
a drop or two will enhance the flavor even further.*

MAKES 2 16-OUNCE SERVINGS

1 frozen banana (page 51)

1 cup frozen chopped spinach

⅔ cup fresh mango, peeled, pitted, and cubed

2 tablespoons hemp seeds

1¾ cups unsweetened almond milk

1 cup ice

sweetener, to taste

Blend all the ingredients together until smooth. Taste, and sweeten as desired.

SUPERFOOD BOOST
Add 1 teaspoon wheatgrass powder
for an even bigger green boost.

PINEAPPLE WATERCRESS

As one of the most powerful salad greens and a well-studied anti-carcinogen, watercress is a nutritional hero, but those benefits can be tricky to obtain. Spicy, peppery, and nipping with flavor, watercress isn't a green that can be "masked" in a smoothie, only balanced out. Here, pineapple and avocado effectively soothe its bite, and adding a little additional sweetener makes this blend especially alluring.

MAKES 2 16-OUNCE SERVINGS

½ cup frozen pineapple

1 cup chopped very ripe pear

¼ cup mashed avocado

1 cup (packed) watercress

½ teaspoon camu powder

1½ cups pineapple juice

2 cups green tea ice
(see page 11)

sweetener, to taste

Blend together all the ingredients, except the ice, until smooth. Add the ice and blend once more until frosty. Taste, and sweeten as desired.

SUPERFOOD BOOST
Add 1 tablespoon chia seeds.

GREEN TEA PEAR

*Between the metabolism-boosting green tea and the filling-yet-low-calorie chia gel,
this smoothie healthfully assists with weight loss in a refreshing way. It's also
the least heavy and lowest calorie recipe in this book.*

MAKES 2 16-OUNCE SERVINGS

3 cups chopped very ripe pear

1½ cups green tea, chilled

1 cup chia gel (page 21)

1 teaspoon wheatgrass powder

sweetener, to taste

Blend all the ingredients together until smooth. Taste, and sweeten
as desired.

SUPERFOOD BOOST
Add 20 drops (or more) of chlorophyll concentrate
to boost energy . . . as well as color.

CHOCOLATE KALE

Some people may not like greens, but almost everyone likes chocolate—and that's all you'll taste in this thick, wonderfully irresistible shake.

MAKES 2 16-OUNCE SERVINGS

2 frozen bananas (page 51)

1 cup ice

❉ 1½ cups (packed) chopped kale

❉ 3 tablespoons cacao nibs

❉ 2 tablespoons cacao powder

1½ cups rice milk (original variety)

sweetener, to taste

Blend all the ingredients together until smooth. Taste, and sweeten as desired.

SUPERFOOD BOOST
Add 2 tablespoons hemp seeds for healthy fats.

MINT CHIP

Tucked beneath a very convincing ice cream-like flavor, a wealth of beneficial spinach awaits you in this smoothie. It's so good it almost makes a person wonder why spinach isn't used in all minty treats. I love how the cacao nibs provide a bit of dark-chocolate crunch without being overpowering.

MAKES 2 18-OUNCE SERVINGS

2 cups frozen spinach

2 cups frozen bananas (page 51)

¼ cup raw cashews

3 tablespoons cacao nibs

2 tablespoons (packed) minced fresh mint leaves

1 teaspoon vanilla extract

2 cups rice milk (original variety)

½ cup coconut water

sweetener, to taste (optional)

Blend all the ingredients together until smooth. Taste, and sweeten as desired.

SUPERFOOD BOOST
Add ¼ teaspoon chlorella powder (or to taste).

GREEN PROTEIN

What happens when two of the most popular types of power blends—protein shakes and green smoothies—join forces? This creamy goodness. Talk about a great lunch, or even invincibly healthy dinner.

MAKES 2 16-OUNCE SERVINGS

⅔ cup chopped celery

⅓ cup dried white mulberries

1½ cups unsweetened almond milk

2 cups (packed) baby spinach

3 tablespoons hemp protein powder

2 tablespoons almond butter

2 cups almond ice (page 11)

sweetener, to taste (optional)

Blend all the ingredients together, except the ice, until smooth. Add the ice and blend once more until creamy. Taste, and sweeten as desired.

SUPERFOOD BOOST
Add extra hemp seeds to taste for even more protein and healthy fats.

LEMON LIME

Let the truth come out: I first made a variation of this slushie-like smoothie as one of the "healthy margaritas" I make from time-to-time (yes, I put superfoods in my cocktails . . . why not?). Tequila-talk aside, this version still has the tart flavor of a margarita, only with more concentrated benefits. You'll definitely want to sweeten this a bit—its citrusy, sour notes are quite prominent. I generally use 15 drops of stevia per blender, and adding a single tablespoon of coconut sugar is a special treat.

MAKES 2 16-OUNCE SERVINGS

3 cups (packed) chopped baby bok choy

2½ cups coconut ice (page 11)

½ teaspoon fresh lemon zest

¼ cup freshly squeezed lemon juice

¼ cup freshly squeezed lime juice

1 cup coconut water

sweetener, to taste

Blend all the ingredients together until frosty and smooth. Taste, and sweeten as desired.

SUPERFOOD BOOST
Add 1 teaspoon wheatgrass powder.

SESAME APPLE

I have a bit of an obsession with tahini in savory recipes—it complements plant-based foods well, and effortlessly offers that little extra "oomph" that a recipe sometimes needs to take it to delicious stardom. Using tahini in smoothies is surprisingly rewarding, as well; here, it meets one of its food friends, kale, in a slightly sweet context.

MAKES 2 16-OUNCE SERVINGS

1 frozen banana (page 51)

2 cups (packed) chopped kale

1 tablespoon unsalted tahini

½ teaspoon ginger powder

1½ cups apple juice

2 cups green tea ice (page 11)

sweetener, to taste (optional)

Blend together all the ingredients, except the ice, until smooth. Add the ice and blend once more until frosty. Taste, and sweeten if desired.

....

SUPERFOOD BOOST
Add ½ teaspoon camu powder.

....

SWEET PEA

Inherently creamy and slightly sweet, both frozen and cooked peas make a wonderful addition to smoothies, and are a good source of protein. This blend is extra cleansing due to its healthy supply of fresh parsley, which is highly alkaline and full of minerals.

MAKES 2 16-OUNCE SERVINGS

¼ cup raw cashews

1½ cups apple juice

1 cup water

2 cups frozen peas

½ cup chopped fresh parsley leaves

1 tablespoon chopped fresh mint leaves

¼ teaspoon camu powder

sweetener, to taste

Blend all the ingredients together until smooth. Taste, and blend in sweetener as desired.

SUPERFOOD BOOST
Add 2 tablespoons hemp protein powder to turn this into a protein-packed green shake.

ROSEMARY ORANGE

From a culinary standpoint, one of the things I most appreciate about smoothies is how easy it is to create truly sophisticated flavor profiles, with about the same effort as doing a load of laundry. This show-stopping blend is a shining example of breathtaking natural flavors working together in harmony.

MAKES 2 16-OUNCE SERVINGS

¼ cup dried white mulberries

¼ cup raw cashews

3 cups baby spinach

2 tablespoons mashed avocado

1 teaspoon orange zest

1½ teaspoons minced fresh rosemary

1½ cups orange juice

2 cups ice

sweetener, to taste

Blend together all the ingredients, except the ice, until smooth. Add the ice and blend once more until frosty. Taste, and sweeten as desired.

SUPERFOOD BOOST
Add ½ teaspoon camu powder.

DOGGIE SMOOTHIE

(a.k.a. FRITZ'S SPECIAL BLEND)

*Yes, not only can you make superfood smoothies for your dog, but they will thank you
for it with many licks and wags! I've been giving my German shepherd, Fritz, green smoothies
since he was a little puppy as a way to pack more nutrition into his food, and he loves them
so much he now dramatically stands at attention when I so much as walk toward the blender.
It goes without saying, green dog smoothies are very flexible, but this one is Fritz's favorite.*

MAKES ABOUT 16 OUNCES

- 2 cups (packed) chopped kale, stems okay to include
- 1 banana
- 1 tablespoon chia seeds
- 1 tablespoon hemp protein powder
- ½ tablespoon peanut butter
- 1 cup water

Blend together all ingredients until smooth. How much you give your pet depends on age, activity level, and size—start small and build from there.

SMOOTHIES AND PETS

There are many foods that are particularly good for dog smoothies, including superfood seeds and oils—such as flax, chia, and hemp—for their anti-inflammatory fats, some fruits—such as bananas and apples—as treats, and any variety of leafy greens, which not only mimic a canine's more intuitive diet (there's a reason dogs eat grass!), but also provide many of the vitamins and minerals that are often skimped on in store-bought formulas or meat-heavy raw diets. A small amount of peanut butter can convince even the pickiest of canines to give something a try.

Note that there are a few common plant foods and superfoods that you should never put into a dog smoothie due to animal sensitivity and/or toxicity. **Never feed your pet the following foods:**

- Avocados
- Cacao/Chocolate
- Grapes/Raisins
- Macadamia nuts
- Tea

RASPBERRY JALAPEÑO

Though they have quite the reputation, the actual flesh of jalapeños doesn't carry much spice, lending only the lightest spark to the taste of raspberries in this recipe. If you like more heat, add a few of the seeds from the pepper to the mixture—just be sure to blend extra well to avoid a surprise sip of fire!

MAKES 2 16-OUNCE SERVINGS

¼ cup Medjool dates, pitted (about 3–4 large fruits)

1 green jalapeño pepper, seeds and stem removed

1½ cups coconut water

1 cup frozen raspberries

1 cup frozen strawberries

1½ cups frozen spinach

1 cup rice milk (original variety)

2 tablespoons freshly squeezed lime juice

sweetener, to taste

Blend together the dates, jalapeño, and coconut water until smooth. Add the remaining ingredients and blend again until frosty. Taste, and sweeten as desired.

....

SUPERFOOD BOOST
Add 1 tablespoon chia seeds.

....

WATERMELON CUCUMBER

Botanical relatives, these two hydrating plants taste even more refreshing when blended together. This smoothie is also a perfect example of how a few drops of stevia can make mild flavors bloom magnificently.

MAKES 2 18-OUNCE SERVINGS

4 cups cubed seedless watermelon

2 cups chopped cucumber, peeled

1½ cups frozen spinach

1 tablespoon chia seeds

1 tablespoon minced fresh basil leaves

1 tablespoon freshly squeezed lime juice

2 cups ice

sweetener, to taste

Blend the watermelon and cucumber together into a juice. Add the remaining ingredients and blend once more until smooth. Taste, and blend in sweetener as desired.

SUPERFOOD BOOST
Add 1 teaspoon wheatgrass powder.

CITRUS ALOE

◊ ◖ ✳

Aloe vera juice (see page 187 for resources), which is excellent for digestion and cleansing, has a very sharp, "clean" flavor that plays well with citrus—my favorite way to drink it. Delightful taste aside, this is a particularly fabulous blend for radiant skin.

MAKES 2 16-OUNCE SERVINGS

1 cup frozen pineapple

1 cup coconut ice (page 11)

¼ cup chopped parsley

1 teaspoon wheatgrass powder

2 tablespoons mashed avocado

2 cups orange juice

¼ cup aloe vera juice

sweetener, to taste

Blend all the ingredients together until smooth. Taste, and sweeten as desired.

....

SUPERFOOD BOOST
Add 1 teaspoon wheatgrass powder.

....

BANANA FENNEL

Anise-like and refreshing, fresh fennel has a way of livening up any green vegetable party it's invited to. Add a little natural fruit sweetness to the mix, and you've got an almost candy-like green smoothie that's guaranteed to wow.

MAKES 2 16-OUNCE SERVINGS

1 cup frozen kale

1 cup diced fresh fennel (bulb only)

2 tablespoons dried white mulberries

1 very ripe banana

2 tablespoons freshly squeezed lemon juice

1 cup apple juice

1½ cups ice

sweetener, to taste

Blend together all ingredients, except the ice, until creamy. Add the ice and blend until frosty. Taste, and sweeten as desired.

SUPERFOOD BOOST
Add 1 tablespoon chia seeds.

RICH & CREAMY

With flavors ranging from classic chocolate to exotic acai, these luscious milkshake-like recipes set the perfect stage for using heavier superfoods like hemp seeds and hemp protein, chia seeds, acai, cacao, and maca. Rich and creamy smoothies often abound with minerals, healthy fats, and protein, turning what tastes like a naughty treat into a nutrition powerhouse. Filling, yet not heavy, these are excellent lunchtime, snack, or even dessert replacements. Many are also perfect for post-workout regeneration.

= FEATURED SUPERFOOD INGREDIENT

BEAUTY   BONE STRENGTH   CLEANSE/DETOX

HEART HEALTH   IMMUNITY   LOW CALORIE   PROTEIN

LUCUMA MACADAMIA

One of my ongoing projects at Navitas Naturals, the superfood company I work with, is developing new superfood smoothie recipes (I know—it's a stretch for me!) for their popular Smoothment campaign (check out the full campaign on their website, smoothment.navitasnaturals.com). This is a version of one of my most beloved blends from that series.

MAKES 2 12-OUNCE SERVINGS

2 cups ice

¼ cup unsalted macadamia nuts

2 large Medjool dates, pitted

¼ cup silken tofu

2 tablespoons lucuma powder

1 tablespoon flaxseed powder

1 tablespoon hemp seeds

1 tablespoon coconut sugar (or stevia, to taste)

¾ cup fresh coconut water

sweetener, to taste (optional)

Blend all the ingredients together until smooth. Taste, and sweeten as desired.

SUPERFOOD BOOST

Add 1 teaspoon wheatgrass powder.

BLUEBERRY MAQUI

*In this smoothie, I love the juxtaposition between the lightness of the ingredients
and the creaminess of the texture. Though I very rarely add sugars like maple syrup into healthy
smoothies, in this case a single spoonful gives the berry flavors that extra-special touch.*

MAKES 2 12-OUNCE SERVINGS

2 cups frozen blueberries

½ cup mashed soft silken tofu

2 teaspoons maqui berry
powder

½ teaspoon cinnamon powder

1 tablespoon maple syrup
(Grade B, if available)

1½ cups coconut water

sweetener, to taste (optional)

Blend all ingredients together until smooth. Taste, and adjust
sweetness if desired.

SUPERFOOD BOOST
Add a large handful of fresh spinach or
kale for extra cleansing benefits.

MAYAN CHOCOLATE

*Though they may not have had blenders, the ancient cultures of Central America often consumed
chocolate in a smoothie-esque form: They ground cacao nibs, nuts, peppers, and spices into a paste,
then watered down the mixture and consumed it as a bitter, cool drink. An homage to the "original"
cacao recipes of the world, this sweeter version is organically powerful and delightfully fiery.*

MAKES 2 12-OUNCE SERVINGS

¼ cup Medjool dates, pitted
(about 3–4 large fruits)

2 tablespoons almond butter

3 tablespoons cacao nibs

1 tablespoon cacao powder

¼ teaspoon cayenne powder

¼ teaspoon cinnamon powder

1 teaspoon vanilla extract

1⅓ cups water

2 cups ice

Blend all the ingredients together, except the ice, until smooth. Add
the ice and blend again until frosty.

SUPERFOOD BOOST
Add 2 tablespoons chia seeds for
additional fiber and healthy fats.

PUMPKIN PIE

Pumpkin puree is inherently an inspired smoothie ingredient: It's creamy, thick, and slightly sweet! This recipe is a fabulous (and healthy) way to enjoy a version of the favorite holiday treat all year round.

MAKES 2 20-OUNCE SERVINGS

1 cup canned pumpkin puree

¼ cup Medjool dates, pitted (about 3–4 fruits)

1 tablespoon almond butter

2 tablespoons hemp seeds

2 tablespoons flaxseeds

1 teaspoon pumpkin pie spice powder

1½ cups unsweetened almond milk

3 cups coconut ice (page 11)

sweetener, to taste (optional)

Blend together all ingredients, except the coconut ice, until creamy. Add the ice and blend until frosty. Taste, and sweeten as desired.

SUPERFOOD BOOST

Add ½ teaspoon wheatgrass powder for a plethora of additional vitamins and minerals.

PISTACHIO CHERRY

Pistachios provide a tremendous amount of sweet, creamy flavor to this blended drink—a real treat. Plus, thanks to the antioxidants in the cherries, goji berries, and even pistachios, this blend is particularly helpful for protecting eyesight.

MAKES 2 16-OUNCE SERVINGS

1½ cups frozen cherries, pitted

¼ cup unsalted pistachios, shelled

¼ cup dried goji berries

1 teaspoon vanilla extract

1 cup water

1½ cups ice

sweetener, to taste (optional)

Blend together all the ingredients, except the ice, until creamy and smooth. Add the ice and blend until frosty. Taste, and sweeten as desired.

....

SUPERFOOD BOOST
Add 1 tablespoon cacao powder.

....

CREAMY CARROT

For my fellow carrot juice-loving friends, this soothing smoothie is just for you. Almost like ice cream, the ingredients blend into delightfully sweet carrot bliss.

MAKES 2 16-OUNCE SERVINGS

1 frozen banana (page 51)

⅓ cup raw cashews

⅓ cup hemp seeds

¾ teaspoon vanilla extract

1½ cups carrot juice

2 cups ice

sweetener, to taste

Blend all ingredients together, except for the ice, until creamy. Add the ice and blend until frosty. Taste, and sweeten as desired.

SUPERFOOD BOOST
Add 1 teaspoon wheatgrass powder for an undetectable green vegetable boost.

BANANA OAT

◈ ✳ ◖◗

Packed with protein, fiber, and nutrient-dense carbohydrates, this filling blend takes "delicious breakfast" to a whole new level. Do note that if it sits for longer than 30 minutes, the smoothie will thicken substantially, although still be tasty.

MAKES 2 16-OUNCE SERVINGS

⅓ cup rolled oats

✳ ½ cup dried white mulberries

2 frozen bananas (page 51)

✳ 3 tablespoons hemp protein powder

1 teaspoon vanilla extract

1½ cups water

1½ cups ice

sweetener, to taste (optional)

Blend all ingredients together until creamy. Taste, and sweeten as desired.

....

SUPERFOOD BOOST
Add 1 teaspoon maqui berry powder
for extra anti-aging antioxidants.

....

SEA BUCKTHORN MANGO

Sea buckthorn juice gives mango a bit of a citrus edge, proving that these two golden fruits definitely belong together. A touch of sweetener enhances their flavors even further, so don't be shy with it.

MAKES 2 16-OUNCE SERVINGS

3 cups frozen mango chunks

2 tablespoons hemp seeds

3 tablespoons sea buckthorn juice

2 cups rice milk (original variety)

1 teaspoon vanilla extract

sweetener, to taste

Blend together all the ingredients until smooth. Taste, and sweeten as desired.

SUPERFOOD BOOST
Add 2 tablespoons chia seeds for additional fiber.

PINEAPPLE MACA

Maca rarely works well with any fruits besides bananas, yet in this recipe, hints of pineapple somehow connect with maca's earthiness and freshen it up with a bit of tropical love.

MAKES 2 16-OUNCE SERVINGS

2 cups frozen pineapple

1½ cups coconut water

2 tablespoons almond butter

1 frozen banana (page 51)

2 teaspoons maca

sweetener, to taste (optional)

Blend all ingredients together until frosty. Taste, and sweeten as desired.

SUPERFOOD BOOST
Add ½ teaspoon camu powder for extra vitamins.

COOKIE DOUGH

Even though there's no real cookie dough in this smoothie, it sure tastes like it! Caramel-like dates, rich and nutty pecans, and cacao nibs with their hint of chocolate blend perfectly with lucuma powder—which has a natural cookie-like flavor—making this smoothie all kinds of fabulous.

MAKES 2 14-OUNCE SERVINGS

¼ cup raw pecans

¼ cups Medjool dates, pitted (about 3–4 large fruits)

1 cup chopped very ripe pear

2 tablespoons lucuma powder

1 teaspoon maca powder

1½ cups almond milk

2 tablespoons cacao nibs

2 cups coconut ice (page 11)

sweetener, to taste (optional)

Blend together all the ingredients, except the cacao nibs and coconut ice, until creamy and smooth. Add the nibs and ice and blend until frosty, leaving the nibs to serve as the "chocolate chips" and add a crunchy kick. Inherently dessert-like, it is unlikely you will need to boost the sweetness, but taste the smoothie and add if desired.

SUPERFOOD BOOST
Add 1 tablespoon chia seeds.

CARAMELIZED BANANA

I adore caramelized bananas because they transform already delicious bananas into something completely decadent with only minor ingredient additions and minimal effort. Even though it's not really an everyday smoothie due to its extra effort, save this blend to eat as a special dessert, or perhaps gift it to that fancy someone you're trying to impress—it's quite the treat.

MAKES 2 12-OUNCE SERVINGS

2 bananas, peeled and sliced
   into ½-inch rounds

1 tablespoon coconut sugar

1 tablespoon coconut oil

1 cup unsweetened almond milk

1 tablespoon maca powder

2 tablespoons chia seeds

3 cups coconut ice (page 11)

sweetener, to taste (optional)

In a medium bowl, dust the bananas with the coconut sugar and toss to coat. Heat the coconut oil in a small sauté pan over medium heat until melted. Add the bananas and cook, flipping occasionally, for 5 minutes, or until the bananas have browned and the sugar has caramelized. Remove from the heat, transfer the contents to a bowl. Pour any remaining liquid from the pan on top of the bananas, and place in the freezer for 15 minutes to chill. When it's time, remove the bananas from the freezer and transfer to a blender. Add the remaining ingredients and blend until frosty and smooth. Being very dessert-like, it is unlikely you will need to boost the sweetness, but taste the smoothie and add some if desired.

....

SUPERFOOD BOOST
Get in a little green by adding 1 teaspoon wheatgrass powder.

....

RASPBERRY ALMOND

Although I have no definite proof, I believe this sweet, comforting smoothie is what raspberries dream about becoming someday while spending their days idling on the vine.

2 cups frozen raspberries

¼ cup Medjool dates, pitted (about 3–4 large fruits)

2 tablespoons almond butter

2 tablespoons acai powder

1 tablespoon cacao nibs

1 teaspoon vanilla

1½ cups coconut water

1 cup ice

sweetener, to taste (optional)

Blend together all the ingredients until smooth. Taste, and sweeten if desired.

SUPERFOOD BOOST
Use dried mulberries in place of the Medjool dates.

GREEN TEA GOJI

Tea and goji berries are almost synonymous in China, where goji grows indigenously. It makes sense that they easily come together in this smoothie, which reminds me of a green tea ice cream. If you can find it, matcha powder (finely milled young green tea leaves) makes a healthy and flavorful addition to this smoothie.

MAKES 2 16-OUNCE SERVINGS

¼ cup raw cashews

1 frozen banana (page 151)

3 tablespoons dried goji berries

½ cup apple juice

1½ cups prepared green tea (chilled)

1 cup ice

sweetener, to taste

Blend together all the ingredients, except the ice, until smooth. Add the ice and blend once more until frosty. Taste, and sweeten if desired.

SUPERFOOD BOOST
Add 1 tablespoon wheatgrass powder.

CREAMY ORANGE

*Tasting like a creamsicle in a glass, even a boast of "amazing"
does not properly describe this blend—it's just heaven.*

MAKES 2 14-OUNCE SERVINGS

¼ cup raw cashews

 ¼ cup hemp seeds

¼ cup Medjool dates, pitted
(about 3–4 large fruits)

1 teaspoon camu powder

2 teaspoons fresh orange zest

1½ cups orange juice

2 cups coconut ice (page 11)

sweetener, to taste (optional)

Blend together all the ingredients until smooth. Taste, and sweeten
if desired.

SUPERFOOD BOOST
Add 1 tablespoon goji berries, which
will enhance the orange color.

MAQUI BANANA

Experience the profound beauty of delicious simplicity.

MAKES 2 14-OUNCE SERVINGS

3 frozen bananas (page 51)

2¼ cups coconut milk (boxed variety)

1 tablespoon maqui berry powder

sweetener, to taste (optional)

Blend together all the ingredients until smooth. Taste, and sweeten if desired.

SUPERFOOD BOOST
Add 1 tablespoon chia seeds.

MACA OAT

My mother is a creature of habit: When she finds something she likes, she makes it a lifestyle. So it came as no surprise when, upon discovering how much she enjoyed a little maca stirred into her morning oatmeal, she began to have it every day. Also unsurprising is how this flavor combo makes an epic smoothie, which indeed makes a fantastic breakfast. And you never know—you may start having it every day!

MAKES 2 14-OUNCE SERVINGS

2 frozen bananas (page 51)

1 tablespoon maca powder

1 tablespoon chia seeds

2 tablespoons rolled oats

2 cups almond milk

⅛ teaspoon cinnamon powder

sweetener, to taste

Blend together all the ingredients until smooth. Taste, and sweeten if desired.

....

SUPERFOOD BOOST
Add ¼ teaspoon chlorella powder (or more, to taste).

....

TAHINI MULBERRY

A combination of two Turkish food gems: tahini and dried white mulberries.
Think peanut butter and jelly—except much *better.*

MAKES 2 16-OUNCE SERVINGS

⅓ cup dried white mulberries

1 banana

2 tablespoons unsalted tahini

1½ cups coconut water

1 tablespoon chia seeds

2½ cups ice

sweetener, to taste

Blend together all the ingredients, except the ice, until smooth. Add the ice and blend once more until frosty. Taste, and sweeten if desired.

SUPERFOOD BOOST
Add 1 tablespoon acai powder.

MULBERRY LAVENDER

The key to using lavender in recipes is a light hand—adding just a little creates a gorgeous pop of flavor, while too much makes a drink taste soapy. You can purchase culinary lavender at specialty food stores, but use it fresh if you have it growing in your yard (just remove the stems and green parts first). If you include maqui berry powder in this recipe, the smoothie will not only taste like lavender, but look the part, too.

MAKES 2 16-OUNCE SERVINGS

⅓ cup dried white mulberries

¼ cup raw cashews

1½ cups unsweetened almond milk

¼ cup soft silken tofu

1 tablespoon chia seeds

2 cups coconut ice (page 11)

1 teaspoon lavender flowers

sweetener, to taste (optional)

Blend all the ingredients together until smooth. Taste, and blend in sweetener as desired.

SUPERFOOD BOOST
Add 1 tablespoon maqui berry powder
to give the smoothie a lavender hue!

CHOCOLATE HAZELNUT

Interestingly, a few drops of almond extract help enhance the natural flavors of the hazelnuts (but if you don't have any on hand feel free to skip it).

MAKES 2 16-OUNCE SERVINGS

¼ cup roasted hazelnuts

1 cup chopped ripe pear

2 large Medjool dates, pitted

2 tablespoons cacao nibs

2 tablespoons cacao powder

1½ teaspoons vanilla extract

⅛ teaspoon almond extract (optional)

1½ cups coconut water

2 cups ice

sweetener, to taste

Blend all the ingredients, except the ice, until smooth. Add the ice and blend again until frosty. Taste, and sweeten as desired.

SUPERFOOD BOOST
Add 1 teaspoon wheatgrass powder for an undetectable green boost.

BLACKBERRY VANILLA

Goodness! This blend's fantastic flavor combines the tastes of homey blackberry pie and classic ice cream. There is, however, one downside to using blackberries in smoothies: They leave behind many of their chewy seeds, which somehow manage to avoid the blades of even the most top-notch blenders. If you're texture-sensitive, you can blend together the blackberries, apple juice, and water first, then strain out the seeds through a sieve before finishing the recipe.

MAKES 2 18-OUNCE SERVINGS

¼ cup raw cashews

2 tablespoons hemp seeds

1 tablespoon lucuma powder

1½ cups apple juice

1 cup water

1½ cups frozen blackberries

½ cup frozen blueberries

sweetener, to taste

Blend together all the ingredients, except the frozen blackberries and frozen blueberries, until smooth. Add the frozen fruit and blend again until frosty. Taste, and sweeten as desired.

....

SUPERFOOD BOOST
Add 1 tablespoon ground flaxseeds.

....

CACAO CREAM

This is a version of my other favorite Navitas Naturals Smoothment recipe. Cacao combined with Brazil nuts tastes like chocolate and peanut butter—need I say more?

MAKES 2 16-OUNCE SERVINGS

¼ cup raw Brazil nuts

¼ cup Medjool dates, pitted (about 3–4 large fruits)

2 tablespoons cacao powder

2 teaspoons maca powder

2 cups unsweetened almond milk

1½ cups ice

1 tablespoon cacao nibs

sweetener, to taste

Blend together all ingredients, except the ice and cacao nibs, until creamy. Add the ice and nibs and blend until frosty. Taste, and sweeten as desired.

SUPERFOOD BOOST
Add 2 tablespoons hemp protein powder.

CACAO MOCHA

Coffee lovers rejoice: those blended, whipped, syruped, fancy-named-accinos just met their homemade superfood match. This concoction of mocha flavor made with raw cacao is wonderfully energizing and dangerously delicious.

MAKES 2 14-OUNCE SERVINGS

⅓ cup raw cashews

¼ cup Medjool dates, pitted (about 3–4 large fruits)

2 tablespoons cacao nibs

1 tablespoon cacao powder

2 teaspoons instant coffee powder (regular or decaf)

2 teaspoons vanilla extract

1½ cups water

3 cups ice

sweetener, to taste (optional)

Blend together all the ingredients, except the ice, until creamy and smooth. Add the ice and blend until frosty. Taste, and sweeten as desired.

SUPERFOOD BOOST
Add 1 teaspoon maca powder to help support adrenal strength and function.

TOASTED COCONUT & MACADAMIA

✳

Although there are a few minor extra steps involved in making this recipe, the results are otherworldly delicious—this is one of my favorite smoothies! Toasting the coconut enhances the flavor, and the coconut ice gives the smoothie a gentle sweetness without adding any refined sugars. In addition to its transcendent flavor, this smoothie also happens to be very beneficial for after exercise due to the electrolyte-rich coconut water and the restorative and energizing maca root. Taste and believe.

MAKES 2 12-OUNCE SERVINGS

¼ cup dried, unsweetened, shredded coconut

¼ cup unsalted macadamia nuts

2 teaspoons maca powder

1½ cups coconut water

2 cups coconut ice (page 11)

In a small skillet, toast the coconut over medium-high heat, stirring constantly to prevent burning, until golden (about 2 minutes). Transfer immediately to a bowl and let cool.

Blend the toasted coconut, macadamia nuts, maca, and coconut water together into a creamy milk base. Once smooth, add the coconut ice and blend until frosty.

··

SUPERFOOD BOOST
Add 1 teaspoon maqui berry powder for anti-aging antioxidants (and a stunningly colored smoothie, to boot).

··

STEALTH BLENDS

To put it nicely, the flavors of many vegetables can be difficult for some people to appreciate, which is why everyone needs a few stealth smoothie recipes under their belt. Pairing what would seem unlikely superfood and vegetable companions, these unique blends keep familiar flavors in the foreground, while leaving their nutritious veggie secrets undetectable. Full of vitamins, minerals, fiber, and antioxidants, these smoothies—perfect for lunch, afternoon snacks, and even dinnertime—are full of plant-based nutrition made from some of nature's more objectionable produce items. Divulging the secret ingredient to others? Entirely optional.

✳ = FEATURED SUPERFOOD INGREDIENT

❀ BEAUTY   ◉ BONE STRENGTH   ❧ CLEANSE/DETOX

♥ HEART HEALTH   ✺ IMMUNITY   ◊ LOW CALORIE   ⬡ PROTEIN

COCONUT SPICE

Full of beta carotene and the vitamins C and E, sweet potatoes make a welcome addition to a healthy lifestyle . . . and a dreamy one to smoothies. Using a canned sweet potato puree (without additives) is a simple way to keep this ingredient on hand.

MAKES 2 18-OUNCE SERVINGS

1 frozen banana (page 51)

1 cup canned sweet potato puree

2 tablespoons unsweetened coconut flakes

2 tablespoons dried white mulberries

2 tablespoons ground flaxseed powder

1 teaspoon cinnamon powder

¾ teaspoon allspice powder

½ teaspoon ginger powder

1 cup coconut milk (boxed variety)

1 cup water

1 cup ice

sweetener, to taste

Blend together all ingredients, except the ice, until creamy. Add the ice and blend until frosty. Taste, and sweeten as desired.

SUPERFOOD BOOST
Add 2 tablespoons hemp seeds.

ACAI (WITH BEET)

The benefits of beets are huge: They help to purify the blood, enhance circulation, and support the kidneys . . . and that's just the beginning. Unfortunately, not everyone likes beets. This recipe leans on the inherent sweetness and creaminess of roasted beets, but is balanced with citrus and acai flavors. A delicious and unique healthy treat.

MAKES 2 16-OUNCE SERVINGS

¾ cup roasted beets (page 142)

2 oranges, peeled, de-seeded, and segmented

1 cup unsweetened almond milk

3 tablespoons acai powder

2 cups ice

sweetener, to taste

Blend together all the ingredients until smooth. Taste, and sweeten if desired.

SUPERFOOD BOOST
Add ½ teaspoon camu berry powder

HOW TO ROAST BEETS

My absolute favorite way to enjoy the heart-healthy beet, roasting produces a delectably tender result, which can be used to make smoothies sweeter without adding sugar, creamier without adding fat, and more beautiful in the most fuchsia of ways. I always make extra roasted beets to have on hand for other culinary treats, like salads or pilafs. They are so delicious, and will keep for up to one week in the refrigerator.

1. Preheat the oven to 400 degrees F. Line a baking sheet or large pan with a layer of aluminum foil.

2. If still attached, remove the leaves and stems from the beet, leaving a half-inch of stem still on the root (do not trim the end of the root). Wash the beets thoroughly to remove any grit, then dry.

3. Wrap each beet tightly in a piece of aluminum foil, like a baked potato, and space a few inches apart on the prepared baking sheet.

4. Roast the beets for 45–75 minutes, or until tender when poked with a fork. Roasting times will vary upon the size of the beets used.

5. Remove the beets from the oven and place, still wrapped in aluminum foil, in the refrigerator for 30 minutes, or until cool to the touch.

6. Once cool, remove the foil. Trim the root and stem ends of the beets, and gently rub the beets to remove the skins. Store in an airtight container in the refrigerator when not using.

RED VELVET CAKE

This profoundly special blend really is reminiscent of the famous cake in terms of flavor, getting its name from the nutritious red beets that make it extra creamy.

MAKES 2 12-OUNCE SERVINGS

½ cup roasted beets (page 142)

¼ cup dried white mulberries

3 tablespoons cacao powder

1 cup unsweetened almond milk

2 cups coconut ice (page 11)

sweetener, to taste (optional)

Blend all the ingredients together, except the coconut ice, until smooth. Add the ice and blend once more until frosty. Taste, and sweeten if desired.

SUPERFOOD BOOST
Add ½ teaspoon camu berry powder for some vitamin C.

CHERRY VANILLA

In actuality, this smoothie probably belongs in the green smoothie section. Yet here it is in the stealth section as it packs in a ton of green vegetables, yet is surprisingly—indeed, stealthfully—not green at all. This smoothie was given the sign of approval by my friend's one-year-old daughter . . . always a good thing.

MAKES 2 16-OUNCE SERVINGS

2 cups frozen cherries

2 cups (packed) baby spinach

1 tablespoon almond butter

2 cups coconut water

½ teaspoon wheatgrass powder

2 tablespoons vanilla extract

sweetener, to taste

Blend together all the ingredients until smooth. Taste, and sweeten if desired.

SUPERFOOD BOOST
Add 1 tablespoon chia seeds.

RASPBERRY PINEAPPLE

*Here's another concoction that is technically a green smoothie (as it contains greens),
but sure doesn't look or taste it! A nice, fruity-flavored stealth blend, it's ideal
for kids, especially with a little stevia added as sweetener.*

MAKES 2 16-OUNCE SERVINGS

- 2 cups (packed) chopped baby bok choy
- 1½ cups frozen pineapple chunks
- ½ cup frozen raspberries
- 1 banana
- 1½ cups coconut milk (boxed variety)
- 1 teaspoon maqui berry powder
- sweetener, to taste

Blend all the ingredients together until smooth. Taste, and sweeten if desired.

....

SUPERFOOD BOOST
Add 1 tablespoon chia seeds.

....

STRAWBERRY BASIL

Basil gives strawberries a lightly floral accent, but that's not the real secret here. Instead, say hello to tomatoes! Strawberries and tomatoes share many of the same flavor notes, which is why incorporating the lycopene-rich beauties in this blend is a seamless addition.

MAKES 2 16-OUNCE SERVINGS

2 cups frozen strawberries

1½ cups cherry tomatoes

¼ cup dried goji berries

2 large Medjool dates, pitted

2 tablespoons mashed avocado

2 tablespoons freshly squeezed lime juice

1 tablespoon (packed) minced fresh basil

1 cup coconut water

sweetener, to taste

Blend all the ingredients together until smooth. Taste, and sweeten if desired.

....

SUPERFOOD BOOST
Add 1 teaspoon maqui berry powder.

....

CHOCOLATE (WITH CAULIFLOWER)

Who knew that steamed cauliflower could make a smoothie so luscious?
Like a rich, naughty chocolate milkshake that's actually very, very nice.

MAKES 2 20-OUNCE SERVINGS

¼ cup Medjool dates, pitted
(about 3–4 large fruits)

3 cups steamed cauliflower

¼ cup cacao nibs

2 tablespoon hemp seeds

1 tablespoon cacao powder

1½ cups rice milk (original
variety)

2 cups coconut ice (page 11)

sweetener, to taste

Blend together all the ingredients, except the ice, until smooth. Add the ice and blend once more until frosty. Taste, and sweeten if desired.

SUPERFOOD BOOST
Add 2 teaspoons maca powder.

BANANA NUTMEG

"With the right flavor combinations, you can hide basically anything in a smoothie," I flaunted to a friend while writing this book. My friend looked at me inquisitively. "Anything?" she asked. "Sure." I nodded. She looked at me, raised an eyebrow dramatically, and replied, "What about . . . Brussels sprouts?" I paused. I didn't know about blending Brussels sprouts. That sounded pretty gross. "Oh sure, even Brussels sprouts. Definitely," I mumbled with feigned nonchalance. "Well, let's see a recipe for it then," she said smugly. Not one to back down from a challenge, I agreed. It took nine tries, many terrible faces, and utilized just about every smoothie trick in the book, but this stealth smoothie is actually quite delicious. So, yes, even Brussels sprouts. Definitely.

MAKES 2 18-OUNCE SERVINGS

2 frozen bananas, (page 51)

❋ 1 cup frozen Brussels sprouts

3 tablespoons almond butter

1½ cups apple juice

1½ cups unsweetened almond milk

❋ 1 tablespoon maqui berry powder

¼ teaspoon nutmeg powder

¼ teaspoon cinnamon powder

sweetener, to taste (optional)

Blend together all the ingredients until smooth. Taste, and sweeten as desired.

....

SUPERFOOD BOOST
Add 1 tablespoon chia seeds for extra fiber.

....

MAQUI GRAPE

One of the first tricks I learned when I was looking to naturalize my diet years ago was to make frozen grapes as a healthy snack, which are quite satisfying and easy to prepare (just wash, dry, remove from the vine, and freeze). Used in smoothies, they add a granita-esque texture, create plenty of natural sweetness, and do a superb job of masking the healthy cabbage found in this superfood blend. It's especially amazing, since "you'll never taste the cabbage" is not something one gets to boast readily.

MAKES 2 12-OUNCE SERVINGS

1 cup shredded green cabbage

2 tablespoons mashed avocado

2 teaspoons maqui berry powder

1½ cups apple juice

2 cups frozen red grapes

sweetener, to taste (optional)

Blend together all ingredients, except the grapes, until smooth. Add the grapes and blend until frosty. Taste, and sweeten as desired.

SUPERFOOD BOOST
Add 1 tablespoon ground flaxseeds.

LUCUMA COCONUT

*This tastes like a perfectly thick coconut smoothie I had once at a small
natural food store in Oregon. I'm pretty sure it didn't have cauliflower in it,
but seeing how easy it is to hide in the blender, now I can't be fully sure . . .*

MAKES 2 16-OUNCE SERVINGS

1 cup frozen cauliflower

1 frozen banana (page 51)

2 tablespoons hemp seeds

3 tablespoons unsweetened
coconut flakes

2 large Medjool dates, pitted

2 tablespoons lucuma powder

½ tablespoon maca powder

2½ cups coconut milk, boxed
variety

sweetener, to taste

Blend all the ingredients together until smooth. Taste, and sweeten
as desired.

SUPERFOOD BOOST
Add 2 tablespoons hemp protein powder.

ACAI ALMOND

It's easy to use a balanced smoothie like this one as a full meal replacement; it's filling, energizing, and highly tasty. If you take a moment to blend this extra well, the broccoli will add to the creamy texture for an even more delectable result.

MAKES 2 14-OUNCE SERVINGS

2 cups frozen broccoli florets

1 frozen banana (page 51)

2 large Medjool dates, pitted

2 tablespoons almond butter

3 tablespoons acai powder

¼ teaspoon vanilla extract

2 cups coconut water

sweetener, to taste

Blend all the ingredients together until smooth. Taste, and sweeten as desired.

SUPERFOOD BOOST
Add ½ teaspoon camu powder.

APPLE (WITH BROCCOLI)

If you have a broccoli-hater in your household, this may just be your best kept secret. Though it packs in a full 3 cups of broccoli, and even some extra-alkalizing chlorella powder, it tastes like apples!

MAKES 2 18-OUNCE SERVINGS

- 3 cups frozen broccoli
- 1 banana
- ½ teaspoon chlorella powder
- ¼ cup freshly squeezed lemon juice
- 1½ cups apple juice
- 1½ cups almond ice (page 11)
- sweetener, to taste (optional)

Blend all ingredients together until smooth and frosty. Taste, and adjust sweetness if desired.

SUPERFOOD BOOST
Adding 1–2 tablespoons hemp protein powder transforms this into a superb protein shake.

PREMIUM BLENDS

This collection of "ultimate" smoothies makes good use of a well-stocked superfood pantry. Packed to the brim with all kinds of superfoods, these blends don't hold back—using the widest range of ingredients, they contain the broadest spectrum of nutrition. A shoe-in as full meal replacements at any time of the day, you can always add more superfoods, such as a handful of spinach or a pinch of camu powder, if needed. These premium blends scream "go for it!" Note: As these recipes were designed to contain an abundance of superfoods, you'll notice there are no recommended superfood boosts in this collection of premium smoothies. Of course, if you'd like to incorporate additional superfoods into any of these recipes yourself, by all means feel free.

✳ = FEATURED SUPERFOOD INGREDIENT

✳ BEAUTY   ☺ BONE STRENGTH   ☙ CLEANSE/DETOX

♥ HEART HEALTH   ✺ IMMUNITY   ◊ LOW CALORIE   ⬡ PROTEIN

KEY LIME

*There's a very smudged and stained little notebook in my kitchen that I use to write down
new recipes. Though I remember making this smoothie—a creamy, citrusy, truly dessert-like treat—
quite well, the only note scrawled in my book about this is a frantic-looking "AMAZING!!!!"
I think I was too busy smoothie-drinking to document anything else.*

MAKES 2 16-OUNCE SERVINGS

2 frozen bananas (page 51)

1 cup coconut ice (page 11)

3 tablespoons unsweetened
coconut flakes

2 teaspoons fresh lime zest

⅓ cup freshly squeezed lime
juice

2 tablespoons hemp seeds

1 tablespoon ground flaxseed
powder

¼ teaspoon camu powder

¼ teaspoon chlorella powder
(and/or 1 teaspoon wheat
grass powder)

1 tablespoon lucuma powder

1 cup coconut milk

½ cup water

sweetener, to taste

Blend all the ingredients together until smooth. Taste, and sweeten
as desired.

....

OPTIONAL
Add 8–12 drops of chlorella concentrate to turn this smoothie a true
"lime" color, as well as boost its alkalinity and cleansing properties.

....

STRAWBERRY

*This brightly flavored, oh-so-satisfying smoothie is a meal in a glass,
with heaps of anti-aging antioxidants of all varieties.*

MAKES 2 18-OUNCE SERVINGS

- 2½ cups frozen strawberries
- ¼ cup dried white mulberries
- 2 tablespoons chia seeds
- 2 teaspoons maqui berry powder
- ½ teaspoon camu berry powder
- ⅓ cup mashed soft silken tofu
- ¼ teaspoon fresh lemon zest
- 2 tablespoons freshly squeezed lemon juice
- 1½ cups unsweetened almond milk
- ¾ cup apple juice
- sweetener, to taste (optional)

Blend together all the ingredients until smooth. Taste, and adjust sweetness as desired.

CHOCOLATE

If you love chocolate, you will adore this smoothie. Super-packed with nutrients and overflowing with chocolate flavor, this creamy blend offers a bona fide healthy excuse to have chocolate at any (or every) meal.

MAKES 2 16-OUNCE SERVINGS

¼ cup large Medjool dates, pitted (about 3–4 fruits)

2 tablespoons mashed avocado

2 tablespoons cacao nibs

¼ cup cacao powder

3 tablespoons hemp protein powder

2 teaspoons maca powder

1 teaspoon vanilla extract

2½ cups coconut water

1 cup ice

sweetener, to taste

Blend all the ingredients, except the ice, until smooth. Add the ice and blend once more until frosty. Taste, and adjust sweetness as desired.

POMEGRANATE CHERRY

Following the classic "tart fruit-meets-sweet fruit" formula for a perfectly balanced smoothie, pomegranates and cherries are natural flavor friends and provide an exceptionally tasty backdrop for some very powerful superfood guests.

MAKES 2 16-OUNCE SERVINGS

1½ cups pomegranate juice

2 cups frozen cherries

1 frozen banana (page 51)

1 tablespoon acai powder

3 tablespoons hemp seeds

1 tablespoon flax powder

1 cup ice

sweetener, to taste (optional)

Blend together all the ingredients, except the ice, until smooth. Add the ice and blend once more until frosty. Taste, and adjust sweetness if desired.

MIXED BERRY

Adding avocado to smoothies gives them an almost gelato-like texture, as seen in this celebratory berry blend.

MAKES 2 16-OUNCE SERVINGS

1½ cups frozen mixed berries

1 cup ice

1 cup chopped ripe pear

¼ cup mashed avocado

⅓ cup goji berries

1 tablespoon flaxseed powder

2 teaspoons maqui berry powder

1½ cups almond milk

sweetener, to taste (optional)

Blend all the ingredients together until smooth and frosty. Taste, and adjust sweetness if desired.

BANANA BERRY

I'd like to think that this superfood blend is a bit of an homage to the most iconic smoothie flavor combo . . . but with all the best ingredients, of course. If you're not using a high-speed blender, you can always add a touch of extra water or coconut milk to blend more easily (this smoothie is extra-frosty).

MAKES 2 16-OUNCE SERVINGS

- 1½ cups mixed frozen berries
- 2 frozen bananas (page 51)
- 3 tablespoons dried white mulberries
- 3 tablespoons hemp seeds
- 2 tablespoons goji berries
- ½ teaspoon camu powder
- 1 teaspoon maqui berry powder
- 2 cups coconut milk (boxed variety)
- 1 teaspoon vanilla extract
- sweetener, to taste (optional)

Blend all the ingredients together until smooth and frosty. Taste, and adjust sweetness if desired.

SESAME HEMP

I'm obsessed with how the tahini gets sweetened by the banana in this blend and becomes like a creamy version of a sesame candy. Protein-packed and mineral-rich, this smoothie is an especially great one for building the body.

MAKES 2 16-OUNCE SERVINGS

1½ cups ice

2 frozen bananas (page 51)

2 tablespoons unsalted tahini

4 tablespoons hemp protein powder

1 teaspoon maca powder

½ teaspoon chlorella powder

½ teaspoon vanilla extract

1½ cups coconut water

10–20 drops chlorophyll extract (optional)

sweetener, to taste (optional)

Blend all the ingredients together until smooth. Taste, and adjust sweetness if desired.

CHOCOLATE MINT

It's a dessert . . . wait, it's a gelato . . . no, it's an extra-energizing superfood smoothie!
This blend definitely falls in the category of "pinch me—this seriously can't taste
so good and actually be health-enhancing." Ah, but it is.

MAKES 2 18-OUNCE SERVINGS

⅓ cup hemp seeds

¼ cup Medjool dates, pitted
(about 3–4 large fruits)

3 tablespoons goji berries

¼ cup cacao powder

2 tablespoons cacao nibs

3 tablespoons (packed) minced
fresh mint

1 teaspoon wheatgrass powder

¼ cup mashed avocado

2 cups coconut water

3 cups coconut ice (page 11)

sweetener, to taste (optional)

Blend all the ingredients, except the ice, until smooth. Add the ice and blend once more until frosty. Taste, and adjust sweetness if desired.

COCONUT

Fresh young Thai coconuts are not something I use as an everyday ingredient. Usually found
in the produce section of health food stores and Asian markets, they can be a little pricey,
and are rather annoying to open. However, they are so epically delicious in smoothies
I simply couldn't contain myself from sharing one—just one — smoothie that contains them.
Curse me, make the smoothie, drink the smoothie, then thank me.*

MAKES 2 12-OUNCE SERVINGS

½ cup fresh young coconut meat

※ 2 tablespoons dried white
    mulberries

※ 2 tablespoons hemp seeds

2 tablespoons lucuma powder

※ 1 tablespoon flaxseed powder

※ 1 teaspoon maca powder

¾ cup fresh young coconut water

2 cups coconut ice (page 11)

sweetener, to taste (optional)

Blend all the ingredients together until smooth. Taste, and adjust
sweetness if desired.

NOTE

Can't find young Thai coconuts? Use ⅓ cup shredded dried coconut
in place of the coconut meat and boxed coconut water in place of
the fresh coconut water. Not as good, but a nice blend nonetheless.

FRUIT PUNCH

Enjoy a classic blend of flavors—strawberry, orange, and banana—that's virtually foolproof in the world of smoothies. Though you'll find this version well stocked with superfoods, it's easy to add even more nutrient-dense goodies in this versatile recipe (fresh greens, for example).

MAKES 2 14-OUNCE SERVINGS

1 cup frozen strawberries

1 frozen banana (page 51)

2 tablespoons hemp seeds

1 tablespoon flaxseeds

1 tablespoon acai powder

1 teaspoon wheatgrass powder

1½ cups orange juice

½ cup coconut water

sweetener, to taste

Blend all the ingredients together until smooth. Taste, and sweeten as desired.

CHAI

A good chai is composed of an orchestra of warming spices, which contrast so nicely with the coolness of a creamy smoothie. Sometimes I'll add extra ice to this blend and eat it with a spoon like ice cream.

MAKES 2 16-OUNCE SERVINGS

3 tablespoons raw cashews

2 tablespoons hemp seeds

2 large Medjool dates, pitted

2 tablespoons cacao nibs

1 tablespoon chia seeds

2 teaspoons maca powder

¼ teaspoon chlorella powder (optional)

1 teaspoon cinnamon powder

1 teaspoon ginger powder

¼ teaspoon cardamom powder

2 cups coconut water

1 frozen banana (page 51)

1½ cups ice

sweetener, to taste (optional)

Blend together all the ingredients, except the frozen banana and ice, until smooth. Add the remaining ingredients and blend again until frosty. Taste, and sweeten as desired.

TROPICAL

The color of this blend looks like an island sunset. To simplify the recipe, you can always use a frozen tropical fruit mix in place of the frozen pineapple and mango.

MAKES 2 16-OUNCE SERVINGS

1½ cups coconut water

1 banana

1½ cups frozen pineapple

¾ cup frozen mango

2 tablespoons dried goji berries

½ teaspoon camu powder

1 tablespoon chia seeds

2 tablespoons hemp seeds

sweetener, to taste

Blend all the ingredients together until smooth. Taste, and sweeten as desired.

OPTIONAL
Turn this into a green smoothie by adding a few handfuls of fresh spinach.

MANGO GINGER

This smoothie provides a milder ginger fix with sweet mango and coconut to balance it out, but if no one's around I like to increase the ginger to epic hot and spicy levels.

MAKES 2 16-OUNCE SERVINGS

2 cups frozen mango chunks

1 tablespoon freshly grated peeled ginger (or to taste)

2 tablespoons unsweetened coconut flakes

⬜ 2 tablespoons goji berries

⬜ 2 tablespoons dried white mulberries

⬜ ½ teaspoon camu powder

1 tablespoon freshly squeezed lemon juice

1 cup coconut milk (boxed variety)

1½ cups coconut water

⬜ 1 tablespoon chia seeds

sweetener, to taste

Blend together all the ingredients, except the chia seeds, until smooth. Add the chia seeds and briefly mix. Taste, and sweeten as desired.

ACAI

Rich and "berry-ful," this smoothie tastes like acai should: luxurious and delicious. Adding a little bit of plant-based fat (avocado) and extra berries enhances the delicate flavor of the acai.

MAKES 2 16-OUNCE SERVINGS

½ cup frozen blueberries

½ cup dried white mulberries

2 tablespoons hemp seeds

3 tablespoons acai powder

1 teaspoon wheatgrass powder

½ cup mashed avocado

2 cups coconut water

2 cups ice

sweetener, to taste (optional)

Blend together all the ingredients, except the ice, until smooth. Add the ice and blend once more until frosty. Taste, and adjust sweetness if desired.

VANILLA ALMOND

I adore this smoothie—there's no other way to put it. If you can get your hands on fresh coconut water (the kind you get out of a freshly cracked, young white coconut), it will take this already amazing smoothie absolutely over the moon. However, if you only have access to a packaged variety, you'll still find yourself a very happy camper. I think this is sweet as is, but you can adjust the sweetness as you see fit.

MAKES 2 16-OUNCE SERVINGS

⅓ cup dried white mulberries

2 tablespoons dried goji berries

2 tablespoons hemp protein

1 tablespoon lucuma powder

3 tablespoons almond butter

2 teaspoons vanilla extract

½ teaspoon camu powder

1½ cups coconut water

2 cups ice

sweetener, to taste

Blend together all the ingredients, except the ice, until creamy and smooth. Add the ice and blend until frosty. Taste, and sweeten as desired.

SUPERFOOD SHOTS

Looking for a to-the-point health boost? Superfood shots get the job done, fast. Basically miniature, highly condensed smoothies, these "shot" recipes are functional powerhouses of body fuel. Because of their focus on functionality, they make use of a few extraneous, extra-potent superfoods and herbs that can be found in health food stores as well as in the Resource Guide (page 187). Excellent for very specific health needs, running-out-the-door moments, and hardcore health enthusiasts, use these highly nutritious mini-blends whenever you need an extra edge.

ENERGY

A sweet and spicy blend that promotes immediate and sustainable energy.

MAKES 2 SHOTS

¼ cup prepared unsweetened yerba mate tea, chilled

1 tablespoon cacao powder

1 teaspoon maca powder

1 tablespoon coconut sugar

pinch of cayenne pepper

Blend all the ingredients together until smooth.

TURBO BOOST
Add an additional ⅛ teaspoon cayenne pepper.

COLD AND FLU FIGHTER

The high amounts of protective vitamin C, immune-enhancing zinc, and anti-viral phytochemicals found in this superfood shot work together to burn away germs. Note that adding oil of oregano (sold as a tincture in the supplement section of most health food stores) makes this shot especially effective, but very intensely flavored!

MAKES 2 SHOTS

¼ cup orange juice

2 tablespoons dried goji berries

2 teaspoons freshly grated peeled ginger

½ teaspoon camu powder

Blend all the ingredients together until smooth. If desired, strain to remove any excess fiber from the ginger.

TURBO BOOST
Add 6–8 drops oil of oregano.

DETOX

Green makes a body clean—especially when combined with toxin-flushing lemon and aloe vera juice. Out with the bad, in with the pure and new!

¼ cup aloe vera juice

2 tablespoons freshly squeezed lemon juice

※ ¼ teaspoon chlorella powder

※ 1 teaspoon wheatgrass powder

4 drops stevia

Blend all the ingredients together until smooth.

TURBO BOOST
Add 10 drops liquid chlorophyll.

BRAIN POWER

Mild and sweet, this blend helps to increase alertness and balance mood with smart fats, brain-friendly antioxidants, and sustainable sugars.

⅓ cup prepared unsweetened green tea, chilled

※ 1 tablespoon acai powder

※ ½ tablespoon chia seeds

½ teaspoon cinnamon powder

1 tablespoon coconut sugar

Blend all the ingredients together until smooth.

TURBO BOOST
Brew 1 ginkgo biloba tea bag in ⅓ cup of hot water, and let steep for 5 minutes before straining. Let the concentrated tea cool, then add to the shot blend.

STRESS RECOVERY

Promote repair and recovery from all kinds of stress—from the physical pains of athletic endeavors to the emotional wear of work and daily life—with adrenal-supporting phytochemicals, relaxing minerals, rejuvenating electrolytes, and anti-inflammatory compounds.

MAKES 2 SHOTS

⅓ cup coconut water

1 tablespoon almond butter

※ 2 teaspoons ground flaxseed

※ 2 teaspoons maca powder

¼ teaspoon turmeric powder

2 drops stevia

Blend all the ingredients together until smooth.

TURBO BOOST
Add 1 scoop plant-based MSM powder, which helps reduce pain and promote tissue repair.

ANTI-AGING

Fight free radicals, repair signs of premature aging, and protect against future damage with a wide variety of powerful antioxidants, lubricating healthy fats, and essential vitamin C defense.

MAKES 2 SHOTS

⅓ cup prepared green tea (unsweetened), chilled

※ 2 tablespoons dried white mulberries

※ 1 tablespoon hemp seeds

※ 1 teaspoon maqui berry powder

※ ¼ teaspoon camu powder

Blend all the ingredients together until smooth.

TURBO BOOST
Add ½ teaspoon minced fresh rosemary.

WHAT HAPPENED TO MY SMOOTHIE?

Superfood smoothies unquestionably taste best right after being blended, when their flavor, texture, and even nutrition, is at its peak. Every day while writing this book, I gave my friends mason jars filled with new recipes for feedback. Yet I always felt the need to preface the bestowed smoothie with, "This was made this morning. It tastes soooo much better right after it's made—please keep that in mind!" If they liked the depreciated smoothie, I knew the fresh version must be awesome.

These are several problems you may encounter with a superfood smoothie that's been allowed to sit for more than a few hours:

Color: Blending ingredients mimics the start of the body's process for breaking down food, just like chewing—which in turn sets up the food to decompose at a faster rate. This is why you'll notice a quick change in color from a fresh smoothie to one that's even just a few hours old. It's a sign that the antioxidants are, well, oxidizing. In other words, benefits are being lost.

Flavor: Flavor can change dramatically for several reasons, one of them being that smoothies often rely on ice. When the ice melts, the overall taste becomes diluted, amplifying flavors previously hidden with stealthy additions. The flavor of a green smoothie that is icy and fresh versus one that has been allowed to sit for a day is an excellent, if sad, example of just how drastic flavor loss can be.

Texture: Perhaps the biggest problem with trying to store superfood smoothies is the textural changes. When icy or frozen ingredients melt, even when stored in the refrigerator, they can turn a perfect, frosty blend of wonder into a flat, thick sludge that may or may not still taste good. Any smoothie that uses dried fruits, such as dried goji berries or dried mulberries, will have the opposite effect, and turn a beautiful pourable beverage into something so thick it's almost gelatinous. Smoothies that use chia and flaxseed will also thicken tremendously, as these super-seeds absorb an incredible amount of water and will "bulk up" within 10 to 30 minutes. Superfood smoothies containing these ingredients have the potential to become a pitiful, strange blend if left around for even a few hours.

STORING SMOOTHIES

A superfood smoothie is a terrible thing to waste. So what are we to do with a smoothie that can't be consumed right away? The good news is that some smoothies, especially creamier ones that contain less fruit, can sometimes last for a few days in the refrigerator, even if they're no longer at their peak for nutritional benefits. For smoothies that contain a lot of fresh fruit, dried fruit, greens, or flax and/or chia seeds, I use the following general guideline for saving them:

0–4 hours, Refrigeration Stage: Directly after being blended, transfer the smoothie to a glass mason jar. Mason jars are my go-to smoothie storage container for several reasons: They're glass (no toxins or bad plastic taste to worry about), they're inexpensive, they come in all different sizes, and they seal extra tightly. Once the smoothie is in your jar, put it in the refrigerator immediately. If you think you may enjoy the smoothie within half an hour, you can even store it in the freezer for a bit to better preserve its texture. Don't forget to give the jar a good, strong shake before drinking—the contents will settle. Most smoothies can withstand being refrigerated for an hour with little variation, and a few hours without changing too drastically.

4–8 hours, Adjustment Stage: This is the beginning of the moody stage for many superfood smoothies. About one out of three smoothies will be absolutely fine during this time period, another third will be in the "not-as-good" category, and the last third will have transformed into something altogether peculiar, as mentioned in the "What Happened to My Smoothie?" on page 180. Luckily, for the smoothies that need it, there's still hope. All that's required is a bit of recipe adjusting—I call it a smoothie refresh—and you don't even have to return to the blender. Simply add a little extra juice (apple works almost every time), coconut water, nondairy milk, or water with stevia (if the sweetness has suffered) directly into your smoothie-filled mason jar. You can also add a couple of ice cubes if they're handy. Then, shake it all up. Voila: Although it may not be as fabulous as at first blend, it's a refreshed smoothie nonetheless.

More than 8 hours, Freezing Stage: There are certainly some smoothies that can withstand two, even three days in the refrigerator. But for some smoothies, especially the green varieties and the ones that contain flax or hemp (which can become bitter when allowed to sit for extended periods), anything over eight hours is simply not an option. If a superfood smoothie cannot be consumed anytime soon, immediately pour it into an ice cube tray and cover with plastic wrap (or use a container that has a cover). When you're ready for a smoothie, simply pop the smoothie cubes out of the tray into the blender, and add additional liquid of your choice. The flavor will change slightly, but the smoothie will still be of benefit. (This technique also a great time-saver for future smoothie-making.)

Also delicious: Pour extra smoothie remainders into ice pop molds for an extra healthy treat!

PART THREE

EXTRAS

MAKING NUT & SEED MILKS

Homemade nut and seed milks couldn't be easier . . . or healthier. Simply blended with water, many types of nuts and seeds transform into a deliciously creamy beverage that can be used just like dairy, while offering beautiful flavor subtleties. New varieties of nut milks are increasingly available in stores, but making them at home offers clear advantages: a fresher, less expensive product with cleaner ingredients (no preservatives needed). A smart addition to natural recipes, homemade nut milks last about a week, refrigerated.

NUT/SEED*	QUANTITY	WATER**	SOAK TIME
Almonds	¼ cup	1¼ cups	6+ hours
Cashews	¼ cup	1¼ cups	2+ hours
Hazelnuts	¼ cup	1¼ cups	6+ hours
Hemp seeds	¼ cup	1¼ cups	1+ hours
Macadamia nuts	¼ cup	1½ cups	4+ hours
Sesame seeds	¼ cup	1 cup	1+ hours
Sunflower seeds	⅓ cup	1½ cups	2+ hours

*Use raw nuts/seeds for best flavor and health. **Water used for blending (not soak water).

METHOD ONE (SLOWER METHOD, BEST PRODUCT)
Soak, then rinse the nuts or seeds in plenty of water (soak water quantity is not important, as long as it covers the nuts/seeds). Pre-soaking ensures easier blending and a smoother milk. Use a blender to mix the soaked ingredients and measured water (see chart) into a smooth cream. Depending on the power of your blender, this can take anywhere from 20 seconds to several minutes. Use a fine mesh sieve or cheesecloth (or nut milk bag if you have one) to strain out any large particulates.

METHOD TWO (FASTER METHOD, THINNER PRODUCT)
Skip the soaking entirely, and blend the raw nuts or seeds with the water. If a smoother viscosity is desired, strain the liquid before using a sieve, cheesecloth, or nut milk bag.

NUT MILK VARIATIONS
For creams: Reduce the water by half. Conversely, use additional water for "skim" milk.
For sweet milks: Blend in a pitted date or two, or add a little stevia.
For flavored milks: Add spices like cinnamon, powders like cacao, or extracts like vanilla.

SUPERFOOD SUBSTITUTION CHEAT SHEET

It happens to the best of us: Ingredients run out, an item is unavailable, or going to the store just seems like too much effort. Fortunately, many (though not all) natural ingredients can be easily substituted. Results may vary per recipe, but in many cases these quick subs will do the trick. Note that some substitutions are non-superfood ingredients.

SUPERFOOD		SUBSTITUTION
Acai Powder	=	Maqui Berry Powder
Cacao Powder	=	Cocoa Powder
Camu Powder	=	Omit From Recipe
Chlorella/Spirulina	=	Wheatgrass Powder*
Dates	=	Raisins
Flaxseeds/Powder	=	Chia Seeds/Powder
Hemp Seeds	=	Sunflower Seeds
Kale	=	Swiss Chard
Mulberries (Dried)	=	Raisins
Pomegranate Juice	=	Cranberry Juice
Raspberries	=	Blackberries
Strawberries	=	Blueberries
Watercress	=	Arugula

*A good multi-greens powder may also be used.

CONVERSION CHART

NON-LIQUID INGREDIENTS (Weights of common ingredients in grams)

INGREDIENT	1 CUP	¾ CUP	⅔ CUP	½ CUP	⅓ CUP	¼ CUP	2 TBSP
Chia Seeds	163 g	122 g	108 g	81 g	54 g	41 g	20 g
Chopped fruits and vegetables	150 g	110 g	100 g	75 g	50 g	40 g	20 g
Dates, chopped	151 g	117 g	100 g	75 g	50 g	39 g	19 g
Goji berries	111 g	83 g	74 g	55 g	37 g	28 g	14 g
Nuts, chopped	150 g	110 g	100 g	75 g	50 g	40 g	20 g
Nuts, ground	120 g	90 g	80 g	60 g	40 g	30 g	15 g

Note: Non-liquid ingredients specified in American recipes by volume (if more than about 2 tablespoons or 1 fluid ounce) can be converted to weight with the table above. If you need to convert an ingredient that isn't in this table, the safest thing to do is to measure it with a traditional measuring cup and then weigh the results with a metric scale. In a pinch, you can use the volume conversion table below.

VOLUME CONVERSIONS (Used for liquids)

CUSTOMARY QUANTITY	METRIC EQUIVALENT
1 teaspoon	5 mL
1 tablespoon or ½ fluid ounce	15 mL
¼ cup or 2 fluid ounces	60 mL
⅓ cup	80 mL
½ cup or 4 fluid ounces	120 mL
⅔ cup	160 mL
1 cup or 8 fluid ounces or ½ pint	250 mL
1½ cups or 12 fluid ounces	350 mL
2 cups or 1 pint or 16 fluid ounces	475 mL
3 cups or 1½ pints	700 mL

RESOURCE GUIDE

INGREDIENTS

NAVITAS NATURALS
Specializes in organic superfoods and more
Find here: Acai powder, cacao powder and nibs, coconut sugar, camu powder, chia seeds and powder, dried goji berries, dried white mulberries, flax powder, hemp seeds, lucuma powder, maca powder, maqui berry powder, raw cashews, wheatgrass powder
Visit: NavitasNaturals.com

GENESIS TODAY
Offers superfood juices, greens powder, and other superfood products
Find here: Sea buckthorn juice, GenEssentials Greens* (a greens powder blend)
Visit: Genesistoday.com

HERBS, ETC.
Offers a large variety of herbal products
Find here: ChlorOxygen chlorophyll drops*
Visit: Herbsetc.com
Indicates brand-name ingredient

MANITOBA HARVEST
Specializes in hemp foods and oils, including hemp protein powder
Find here: Hemp Pro 70* (a high-protein, water-soluble hemp protein powder that works incredibly well in smoothies)
Visit: Manitobaharvest.com

MOUNTAIN ROSE HERBS
A source for buying bulk organic herbs, spices, and essential oils
Find here: A variety of culinary and medicinal herbs and spices
Visit: Mountainroseherbs.com

NUNATURALS
Carries stevia products
Find here: Liquid, powdered, and even flavored stevia
Visit: Nunaturals.com

SAMBAZON
A source for acai
Find here: Frozen acai packs
Visit: Sambazon.com

VEGA
A source for chlorella powder and other supplements
Find here: Chlorella powder, Maca powder
Visit: Myvega.com

KITCHEN TOOLS

CUISINEART
Find here: Quality mid-range blenders
Visit: Cuisineart.com

GLASS DHARMA
Find here: Reusable glass drinking straws
Visit: Glassdharma.com

OXO
Find here: Ice cube trays with lids
Visit: Oxo.com

TOVOLO
Find here: BPA-free, silicon ice cube trays
Visit: Tovolo.com

VITAMIX
Find here: High-speed blenders
Visit: Vitamix.com

REFERENCES

Ad Hoc Panel of the Advisory Committee on Technology Innovation, Board on Science and Technology for International Development, National Research Council. *Lost Crops of the Incas: Little-Known Plants of the Andes with Promise for Worldwide Cultivation*. Washington D.C.: The National Academies Press, 1989.

Bartimeus, Paula, Charolette Haigh, Sarah Merson, Sarah Owen, and Janet Wright. *Natural Wonderfoods*. London, UK: Duncan Baird Publishers, 2011.

Basu A, Penugonda K. "Pomegranate Juice: A Heart-Healthy Fruit Juice." Department of Nutritional Sciences, Jan. 2009. http://www.ncbi.nlm.nih.gov/pubmed/19146506.

Best, Ben. "Phytochemicals as Nutraceuticals." *Science News*. http://www.benbest.com/nutrceut/phytochemicals.html#anthocyanins.

Bittman, Mark. *Leafy Greens*. New York, NY: Macmillan, 1995.

Clum, Dr. Lauren, and Dr. Mariza Snyder. *The Antioxidant Counter*. Berkley, CA: Ulysses Press, 2011.

Coates, Wayne, PhD. *Chia: The Complete Guide to the Ultimate Superfood*. New York, NY: Sterling, 2012.

Ley, Beth M., Ph.D. *Maca: Adaptogen and Hormonal Regulator*. Detroit Lakes, MN: BL Publications, 2003.

McGee, Harold. *On Food and Cooking: The Science and Lore of the Kitchen*. New York, NY: Scribner, 2004.

Raloff, Janet. "Chocolate as Sunscreen." *Science News*. http://www.sciencenews.org/view/generic/id/7437/title/Food_for_Thought__Chocolate_as_Sunscreen.

Raloff, Janet. "Prescription Strength Chocolate, Revisited." *Science News*. http://www.sciencenews.org/view/generic/id/7075/title/Prescription_Strength_Chocolate%2C_Revisited.

"Vitamin C and Skin Health." Linus Pauling Institutue at Oregon State University. http://lpi.oregonstate.edu/infocenter/skin/vitaminC/index.html.

Wolfe, David. *Superfoods: The Food and Medicine of the Future*. Berkley, CA: North Atalantic Books, 2009.

ACKNOWLEDGMENTS

Anyone can make a smoothie, but it takes a village to create a smoothie book. I humbly acknowledge the tremendous impact of the following individuals who generously contributed their energy to this project:

Thank you first and foremost to Brendan, for giving me endless support and love, and for enthusiastically sipping smoothies with me time and time again. And thank you for sharing your story—which has already inspired so many and will continue to do so—in the foreword.

Thank you to my family, Mom, Dad, and Nama, for your waterfall of sincere you-can-do-it's. I absolutely used every last one of them.

A massive thank you to everyone at Sterling for giving this book such a pride-worthy treatment: Sasha Tropp for your capable care and beautiful literary makeover, Jennifer Williams for all your enthusiastic supervision, Christine Heun, for your gorgeous design and layout, Elizabeth Mihaltse for the inspired cover, and Kim Marini for herding this project every step of the way.

Thank you to Marilyn Allen for bringing this entire journey to fruition.

Thank you to Carolyn Pulvino and Judy Alexander for lending your gifted artistic sensibilities to creating the best little smoothie benefit icons ever.

A huge thank you to the talented Oliver Barth, for your magical photographs that capture the energy and passion of a natural lifestyle.

Thank you to my beautiful group of friends who both humored me with "smoothie talk" and offered valuable recipe feedback.

Lastly, thank you to the entire Navitas Naturals team for supporting me, not only with your incredible superfoods products, but also with the opportunity to work with a company whose people and products I respect so much.

Love you guys,
Julie

SMOOTHIES BY BENEFIT INDEX

Flavor may be the language of smoothies, but the copious underlying benefits tell the whole story. Use this directory to quickly find smoothies that specifically address the demands of your lifestyle.

✳

BEAUTY

These smoothies contain ingredients that boast notable quantities of "beauty nutrients," such as vitamin C (essential for the synthesis of collagen and an anti-inflammatory), essential fatty acids, and anthocyanin antioxidants for skin protection.

BONE STRENGTH

Enjoy these smoothies for their calcium-rich superfoods.

Acai	173	Ginger Pear	78	Sesame Apple	96
Apple (with Broccoli)	154	Green Protein	92	Sesame Hemp	163
Banana Oat	115	Green Tea Goji	123	Strawberry	158
Blueberry Goji	59	Green Tea Pear	88	Strawberry Chamomile	48
Cacao Cream	134	Lemon Lime	94	Sweet Almond	86
Caramelized Banana	120	Mango Coconut	84	Tahini Mulberry	129
Carrot Cardamom	73	Mango Ginger	172	Tropical	170
Chai	169	Mulberry Lavender	130	Vanilla Almond	175
Cherry Vanilla	144	Raspberry Peach	60	Watermelon Acai	52
Chocolate Hazelnut	131	Red Velvet Cake	143	Watermelon Cucumber	103
Chocolate Kale	89	Rosemary Orange	99		
Cucumber Mint	81	Sea Buckthorn Fig	68		

CLEANSE/DETOX

Smoothies that are particularly helpful in flushing the body of toxins and raising alkalinity.

Acai	173	Fruit Punch	167	Rosemary Orange	99
Apple Arugula	82	Ginger Pear	78	Sesame Apple	96
Apple (with Broccoli)	154	Green Protein	92	Sesame Hemp	163
Banana Fennel	105	Green Tea Pear	88	Strawberry Chamomile	48
Banana Romaine	77	Key Lime	157	Strawberry Cucumber	72
Chai	169	Lemon Lime	94	Strawberry Kombucha	58
Cherry Vanilla	144	Lucuma Lime	85	Sweet Almond	86
Chocolate Kale	89	Mango Coconut	84	Sweet Pea	97
Chocolate Mint	164	Mint Chip	91	Watermelon Cucumber	103
Citrus Aloe	104	Pineapple Watercress	87		
Cucumber Mint	81	Raspberry Jalepeño	102		

HEART HEALTH

These smoothies are made with superfoods that have been shown in clinical trials to promote cardiovascular health.

Acai	173	Cranberry Orange	62	Peaches & Cream	65
Acai Almond	153	Creamy Carrot	114	Pistachio Cherry	112
Acai (with Beet)	140	Creamy Orange	124	Pomegranate Cherry	160
Apple Arugula	82	Fruit Punch	167	Pomegranate Orange	57
Banana Berry	162	Grapefruit Pomegranate	70	Pumpkin Pie	111
Banana Nutmeg	150	Green Tea Goji	123	Raspberry Almond	122
Blackberry Vanilla	132	Green Tea Pear	88	Raspberry Peach	60
Blueberry Maqui	108	Honeydew Maqui	47	Raspberry Pineapple	145
Cacao Cream	134	Key Lime	157	Red Velvet Cake	143
Cacao Mocha	135	Lucuma Coconut	152	Rhubarb Mint	64
Caramelized Banana	120	Lucuma Macadamia	107	Sea Buckthorn Mango	116
Carrot Cardamom	73	Maca Oat	128	Strawberry	158
Chai	169	Mango Chili	75	Strawberry Kombucha	58
Chocolate	159	Mango Coconut	84	Sweet Almond	86
Chocolate (with Cauliflower)	148	Mango Ginger	172	Tahini Mulberry	129
Chocolate Hazelnut	131	Maqui Banana	127	Tropical	170
Chocolate Kale	89	Maqui Grape	151	Vanilla Almond	175
Chocolate Mint	164	Mayan Chocolate	110	Watermelon Acai	52
Coconut	166	Mint Chip	91	Watermelon Cucumber	103
Coconut Goji	63	Mixed Berry	161		
Coconut Spice	139	Mulberry Lavender	130		
Cookie Dough	119	Mulberry Plum	67		

IMMUNITY

These are great sources of nutrients that fight disease, like vitamin C and zinc, and/or contain superfoods renowned for having anti-viral, anti-bacterial, or anti-fungal activity.

Apple (with Broccoli)	154	Lemon Lime	94	Raspberry Pineapple	145
Banana Berry	162	Mango Chili	75	Rhubarb Mint	64
Blueberry Goji	59	Mango Ginger	172	Rosemary Orange	99
Cantaloupe Peach	69	Maqui Berry Peach	53	Sea Buckthorn Carrot	55
Carrot Cardamom	73	Mixed Berry	161	Sea Buckthorn Fig	68
Chocolate Mint	164	Orange Goji	51	Sea Buckthorn Mango	116
Coconut Goji	63	Peaches & Cream	65	Strawberry	158
Cranberry Orange	62	Pineapple Maca	117	Strawberry Basil	147
Creamy Orange	124	Pineapple Papaya	56	Sweet Pea	97
Grapefruit Pomegranate	70	Pineapple Watercress	87	Tropical	170
Green Tea Goji	123	Pistachio Cherry	112	Vanilla Almond	175
Key Lime	157	Pomegranate Orange	57		

LOW CALORIE

These smoothies contain approximately 225 calories—or less!—per serving.

Acai (with Beet)	140	Grapefruit Pomegranate	70	Red Velvet Cake	143
Acai Pumpkin	50	Green Tea Goji	123	Strawberry Chamomile	48
Apple Arugula	82	Green Tea Pear	88	Strawberry Cucumber	72
Apple (with Broccoli)	154	Honeydew Maqui	47	Strawberry Kombucha	58
Banana Romaine	77	Lemon Lime	94	Sweet Almond	86
Blueberry Goji	59	Maca Oat	128	Watermelon Acai	52
Blueberry Maqui	108	Maqui Berry Peach	53	Watermelon Cucumber	103
Cantaloupe Peach	69	Mulberry Plum	67		
Citrus Aloe	104	Pistachio Cherry	112		
Cucumber Mint	81	Pomegranate Orange	57		

PROTEIN

Smoothies with 10 grams or more of protein per serving.

Banana Oat	115	Creamy Orange	124	Sesame Hemp	163
Chocolate	159	Green Protein	92	Sweet Pea	97
Creamy Carrot	114	Rhubarb Mint	64	Vanilla Almond	175

INDEX